AF322632

Also by Wes Young

Reaching Sol

ONE STORY, BUILDING

ONE STORY, BUILDING

A Memoir on the Power of Story

WES YOUNG

Wes Young Writer

One Story, Building
A Memoir on the Power of Story
By Wes Young
wesyoungwriter.com

ISBN: 979-8-218-34399-6 Hardback
eISBN: 979-8-218-34400-9 eBook

Library of Congress Control Number: 2024900228

For Robin, my life's best chapter.

Contents

Introduction

One lazy day during my junior year of high school, the teacher gave us a free period to do as we pleased while she worked at her desk. Our boredom eventually gelled into a game of charades. We wrote our own clues on scraps of paper and placed them, facedown, onto a desk. Whoever's turn it was drew a clue and acted it out—silent or talking, we didn't much care.

"Horse?"

"Yeah."

"The principal!"

"Totally."

And so on like this for a while, until eventually it was time to replenish the clues. What I did next embarrasses me terribly. I wrote my own name on one of the scraps and put it secretly in the pile. All the wearisome anxieties of teenage insecurity are represented by that simple, selfish act.

Wes Young. Who am I? And, equally important to me at the time: who am I to them? I wanted feedback, and here I'd stumbled into a unique mirror-mirror on the wall.

If this action was telling, the next bit told even more. A classmate eventually drew the card with my name on it.

I froze, hoping he wouldn't recognize the handwriting. He didn't. Neither did he start acting. There was an awkward pause, an eager anticipation among the competitive crowd of guessers, a quick chuckle, and—nothing.

"I don't know," he finally said. "I mean, I don't know what to do."

I should have seen this coming. Had I drawn the card myself, even I couldn't have acted it out, for I didn't know what *self* of mine there was to act. One might as well have told a liquid to *Shape up!* as tell a young Wes Young to be himself. In those days, my fluid personality, like so much water, knew only how to mold to its surroundings and then reflect like a pool what was already there. But a boy is meant to be a man, not a pond, and I was a man drowning in a sea of too many personality options, too many imitations. In truth, a charade actor who drew my name in those days would do well to check the last movie I'd watched or book I'd read to find out how to be me—if one could rightly call it me. What my real self was, even I did not know.

To be clear, mine was a happy childhood. Good home, great parents. This isn't that sort of memoir. But even in the best of circumstances, growing up is a complex road.

Also, I am not famous. I have neither climbed Everest nor won the World Series. My life might be of regional or personal or comical interest, but that's all. The point, though, is that it provides a convenient and convincing bit of evidence for the argument of this book. A case study is more about the theory being proven than the person, the "case," being studied. So too with this memoir. I use myself because I am a subject I know intimately and have full access to. Other cases might equally work (I doubt any could work better), but their stories are not mine to tell. I am shy about writing of others in any identifiable way, and have deliberately avoided it in this book.

This memoir explores the power of narratives in our world, and shows the particularly strong influence they had in shaping my *self*, especially in the formative years from two to twenty. Humans crave story. A child is born into a world he knows not, and parents give him context through story. An amnesiac wakes in his ward, knowing nothing and nobody, until a loved one tells him the story. Characters, whether fact or fiction, live out their lives on book pages and TV screens, lending context and meaning to our own waking narratives. In my life, I think they gave an inordinate amount of context.

Stories were always the key that fit my lock. I loved them. As a kid, when the Atlanta Braves had a rain delay, and the local cable network filled the slot with *The Andy Griffith Show*, I rejoiced. To this day, I'd rather watch *Field of Dreams* than an actual baseball game. Stories were and are the currency of my mental exchanges, often even surpassing logic. For instance, if I have a load of cold groceries in the trunk of my car and am worried that a stop at the library might take too long, my mind does not go to anything so logical as the science of milk and eggs, pasteurization and salmonella. Instead, it reverts naturally to a narrative: *If I had bought these at a grocery in Warner Robins, I wouldn't think anything of a thirty-minute commute home.* Or again, *If I suffered a flat tire and had to change it, I wouldn't throw out my groceries because of the delay.* And so, thus convinced, I stop at the library.

As a kid, I did not recognize this story potency even when it was right in front of me. In truth, it's an easy thing to miss because stories are by nature transparent. They are lenses. I remember once, as a kid, falling headlong into a season of science. It was a passion that lasted several years, and seemed clearly my life's calling. I would be a scientist. I would invent and experiment. I would, best of all, have a laboratory. Not satisfied to wait until adulthood, I began my experiments right away. I acquired toy test tube kits and log books and all the typical paraphernalia of a dreamy young scientist. For one experiment, I tested a hypothesis I'd formed about objects in motion—we'd been studying Newton in science class at school. I proposed that an object moving one direction and then reversing and going the opposite direction must first, if only for a microsecond, stop entirely.

For my experiment, I hung Dad's 8mm video camera above the wooden desk in my room. I aimed it downward so as to record the flat surface from a bird's-eye angle. I then took an object and slid it forward and backward on the desk as the camera filmed. I did it several times slowly, then several times quickly. Afterwards, I reviewed the tape on the little box television we kept upstairs. I still remember that recording, not so much because it proved anything about motion—it didn't—but because of how blind I was to something so obvious. The object I chose for the back-and-forth slide happened to be a book, and more than that, it was Mary Shelley's *Franken-stein*. I tell you truly, I did not pick that object deliberately, but my subconscious must have been at work. The fact is, my science kick in those days was almost wholly attributable to my reading and watching *Frankenstein*. I was obsessed with that story, and there, mid-experiment, was the mystery right in front of me. I saw nothing, for I had not yet learned to see stories as stories.

Narratives were uniquely cloaked for me because I was eventually to become a storyteller myself, and the writer-calling is peculiarly hard to spot. Were I called to be, say, a baseball player or a fireman, then we'd have recognized the telltale tendencies easily and early.

"Man, that boy just won't stop throwing the ball around, will he?" or "He sure likes those toy fire trucks, doesn't he?" But to be called to storytelling, this is a path fraught with one red herring after another. Neither the kid nor those closest to him see it. One month he plays at ship captain or submarine commander. "Perhaps he ought to join the Navy." The next week he is a secret agent. "He should try the FBI." Then a scientist. Then a musician, hockey player, fisherman, golfer, gangster, and school teacher. On and on it goes, with his passions and pseudo-callings ever changing depending on what book he most recently read or what movie he most recently absorbed. He's like Barney Fife after the Glenn Ford movie played at the Mayberry theater—the very next day demanding a security check at the Mayberry Bank! I totally get that, and will only add that in life it's even more diverse: Glenn Ford saving the bank one week, John Wayne robbing it the next. Such a boy seems mercurial and flighty, and he is, but the answer is as solid as it is elusive: "He loves stories. He's a storyteller."

Imagine, by way of analogy, a kid whose actual calling is to become a telescope maker. Years go by, and everyone misses it. They think for a while that he loves stars, will make a fine astronomer, for he keeps looking at the sky through his telescope. Then later that he loves ships, will make a great sailor, for he keeps staring at the sea's horizon. Or the moon, or the mountains, or the deer across the meadow. Because a telescope is, by nature, a thing meant for viewing other things, identifying an interest in telescopes themselves is uniquely difficult. So too with stories, which are not any one thing, but are humanity's scope for viewing and contextualizing all things. Unseen, yet through them, all else seen. "Story" itself, and the hands that craft it, are as invisible as glass. Think about it, can you name the screenwriter of the last movie or show you watched? Yet these invisible hands, typing away at their keyboards, are running the world.

They certainly shaped my life, as you will see. The power of narratives on my young self was so intoxicating that I came of age as a sort of multiple personality, oil and water and two dozen other streams besides, all unmixing.

Unmixing, but not unbridged. Woven through this memoir, let the reader understand, is the One Story that differed in substance from all the others, the one that eventually overwhelmed and redeemed them all.

This account is entirely true, as I remember it.

PART I

Motion pictures have a very definite place in the fabric of community life, and an important role to perform. They lift the dull cares and worries of everyday life from the minds and shoulders of the masses, and for an hour or so transport them to a make-believe world outside themselves, thereby relaxing and refreshing the mind and body.

—FROM THE SOUVENIR PROGRAM FOR THE GRAND OPENING OF THE VOGUE THEATRE IN COCHRAN, GEORGIA, AUGUST 27, 1951

20,000 Leagues

My family's one childhood pilgrimage to Disney World was marked, beyond anything else, by a single ride: 20,000 Leagues Under the Sea Submarine Voyage. The attraction featured actual, half-submerged *Nautilus* submarines moving along underwater tracks. Inside the sub, below the waterline, passengers sat in two narrow rows, backs to the middle, faces toward the portholes. I loved this ride. Through the watertight glass I saw undersea divers, sunken shipwrecks, cases of golden treasure, and, of course, a giant squid. It was the film come to life, an immersion into the world of Nemo. This attraction ended its twenty-three-year operation in 1994, but it wasn't for lack of enthusiasm from this seven-year-old. I rode and re-rode and re-rode that ride until the employees probably began to wonder what I was up to. And my parents, having paid good money for a day at Disney, had to be wondering if we would ever actually see the rest of the park.

"Wes, how about Dumbo?"

"Or Peter Pan?"

"Or *anything* else?"

To which I replied, pointing at the submarines, "Again!"

Even a detour to the restroom was too much delay for me.

This led, unsurprisingly, to our discovery that the theme park version of Nemo's ship had no "head," no toilet. Mid-ride, well out to sea, I told my dad the bad news: "I really need to go to the bathroom."

Yaaargg.

The scenes out the portholes were the same as the first dozen rounds, but now all I could think about was getting relief. I shook my feet, crossed my legs, uncrossed them again, loosened my belt, tried different positions in the seat—all of little help. When that ride finally reached its dock, my dad and I executed an Abandon Ship maneuver that would have made any admiral proud. I was soon on dry land and rushing to a nearby facility, thankfully maintaining dry pants.

From Our Disney World Trip

I was obsessed with that ride because I was obsessed with that story. I first met Jules Verne's *20,000 Leagues Under the Sea* through a small green paperback—one of those wonderful Illustrated Classic Editions that Moby Books made so popular with people of my generation. I found it on my grandmother's bookshelf, and carried it with me everywhere. I was first grade or so at the time, and not smart enough to understand it fully, but I read what I could and soaked in all the pictures. Around this same time, I was also introduced to Walt Disney's 1954 screen adaptation of the story, and there the hook was set. Time and again I pulled that black VHS from its blue cardboard sleeve, watching and rewatching. It became a well-worn treasure in my childhood home.

No doubt my parents and my brother were good and tired of it after the first dozen replays, but somehow I couldn't get enough. I watched it so much that I could repeat large portions of the script verbatim—I still can. I didn't know what it was that drew me back and back again, and I didn't ask. In those days, the thought process was short and simple: I like this, so I'll do this. There was no dissecting of what exactly it was I liked about it, or why it was working in me and on me. No thought to the method or mechanism, and certainly not to the makers behind the scenes, but only to the feeling evoked. I somehow saw myself in this story, and that was strong tonic.

20,000 Leagues was the reason I started playing the piano. Captain Nemo and his golden pipe organ fascinated me, and I found myself on Sundays lurking around the organ at the back of our little one-story church building. Our church's organist played an electric organ, nowhere near as glamorous as Nemo's, but still it had two rows of keys, and I loved that. I'm not sure she liked being stared at by this peculiar little boy whom she barely knew, but she was a good sport about it, and eventually let me strike a few notes. I was intoxicated.

"How does someone learn to play the organ?" I asked.

"You start with the piano," she explained. "You have to learn the piano first."

That's all it took. For years afterward, I pedaled my bike to piano lessons with a teacher on the far side of our neighborhood, and I did eventually get to play a few songs on our church's organ.

But piano lessons and theme park rides were only residual tremors. The seismic center was strictly nautical. It manifested itself in the waking world when I first discovered sailing. This was fifth grade or so at a 4-H summer camp at Rock Eagle. The camp offered daily breakout sessions, and we campers could sign up for this or that class, depending on our interests. They had all sorts of things to choose from—archery, crafts, canoeing, and so forth. I ended up with canoeing, but as I was walking toward the lake, a fellow from my county caught up to me. He panted out a proposition: "Wes, can we trade cards? I want to do canoeing."

"What's yours?" I replied, suspiciously.

"Sailing."

"Sure, whatever," I said, wholly unaware of the far-reaching effect of that simple decision.

I headed for my new destination knowing nothing and no one. The sailing group gathered along the shore of Rock Eagle Lake on a sandy patch that made a sort of beach. The sailboats were lined neatly on the sand, completely out of the water, and their sails flapped in the easy breeze, pointing downwind. It was a small but tidy fleet—clean hulls, white and flat, probably made by Sunfish. Each boat had one sail, a tiller with an extension rod, a cockpit meant for two, a mainsheet unassisted by pulleys or cams, and a wooden daggerboard that dropped through a slot in the center of the boat.

Our sessions started not on a boat but on the beach. Our instructor stood on the hot sand with the midday summer sun blazing overhead and went over the terms and rules we needed to know. Boat part names comprised the largest portion of the curriculum. Bow, stern, rudder, tiller, mast, gooseneck assembly, mainsheet, daggerboard. I was happy to learn, but also impatient to get on the water. One, because of the heat, but two, because already I sensed in those raised sails something ancient and mysterious, some connection to the sailors who crossed oceans and brought back tales of sea monsters. The men who threw harpoons at the glowing *Nautilus*, they were sailors. This felt right.

Thankfully, we were soon put in pairs and assigned a boat. I did not know the kid partnered with me, but we introduced ourselves to one another and dragged our vessel into the shallow water along the beach. The instructor explained how we were to divide labors aboard ship. Whoever sat forward in the cockpit was in charge of operating the mainsheet—that's the line that pulls in or lets out the mainsail, essentially serving as the throttle. Whoever sat aft was in charge of the tiller—the stick that steers the boat. One at a time, and no doubt awkwardly, we climbed into the cockpit. We did not yet lower the daggerboard, which was a piece of beautifully varnished wood that ran through the center of the boat and deep into the water. The lake was shallow near shore, and the instructor told us to sail out a bit before lowering. "First halfway down," he taught us, "then all the way. And be sure to pull it back up as you come back to the beach."

My crewmate and I sat in our boat, ready and nervous, and hauled in the mainsheet. The boat did not gradually rise up to speed as I expected. Instead, it shot out like a jet ski, from no speed to full speed almost immediately, and that simply by hauling in the sail. My first response was to feel wholly out of control, like one's first time on a horse. Thankfully, the wind was soft that day, so our horse stayed at an easy trot.

We quickly learned how to steer, and also how to scramble to a daggerboard. "Get it down! Get it down!" From our tutorial on the beach, we'd surmised that a centerboard was the only thing that kept a sailboat from immediately capsizing, and even if we overestimated the danger of our situation, we took no chances. "Get it down!"

In truth, we learned all of this, the sheet and tiller and board, in an instant. We had to. And as we found our groove, we looked back in amazement at the receding coast. Canoeing immediately and forevermore struck me as silly, inadequate, and inefficient. I was sold on sailing. Our boat skipped across the water like a dead thing come to life, and the wind did all the work.

So speedily did we cross the lake that we soon had to learn how to turn—a tricky business for us landlubbers. Thankfully, we managed it without capsizing. Back we went, and then forth, and back again, in the manner of all sailors on small seas.

I cannot remember which job I took on our first outing, which is a shame really, because this would tell whether my first touch of sailing fever came through that tightening of the tiller as the moving water applies pressure, or if it came through the clenching fist on the mainsheet as the wind tries to snatch it away. Both are, even to this day, strong tonic. I was instantly hooked. It was on this little outing on this little lake that I first felt the reverie of a canvas filling with wind, the bewilderment that must have overjoyed early man when his modified canoe first moved without paddling.

My crewmate was having fun, I'm sure, but I doubt he had any idea what was going on in the mind of his copilot. Or to put it another way, as he crossed and recrossed that little lake, he had no way of knowing that I was crossing and recrossing the South Pacific. I was Ned Land, in search of a sea monster. I was Captain Nemo, at home in my element. Yes, the invisible, internal transformation had taken place. The story had manifested itself in the waking world, and none else on my little *Nautilus* knew.

For a good while we sailed around and around, having our fun—he in reality and I in my mind. Eventually, though, we wanted more. In this way we discovered the fun of friends, the excitement of the armada. If one boat is good, then two boats are great. We aimed for the others, who were, like us, darting this way and that across the lake. What a thrill it was to pass close to a neighboring vessel, novices skimming by novices, all riding the same wind. The narrower the escape the better—a Blue Angels stunt show on the water.

We cut closer and closer with each new pass. Eventually, of course, we collided. Our bow plowed right through the cockpit of another vessel, striking them broadside, ramming speed, *Nautilus* style. Had our ships been built with higher gunwales, this might have done some damage, but Sunfishes are more like surfboards than boats, so our bow simply skipped over the other's low sidewall and sent us laughing, rather than to Davy Jones's locker.

More sailing and more laughing filled the afternoon, round the lake again and again until finally we brought her to the shallows, lifting the daggerboard halfway, then all the way. We ran her up on the white sands of New Guinea—I mean, Putnam County. The class was over, the voyage ended, but my heart never really made the beach that day. Waves and wind, vessels and voyages, these were my story now.

I craved a ship of me own, and began looking and longing for any and all boats. I spotted them parked in backyards or under carports. I developed a disdain for those incomprehensible, ungrateful adults who owned boats but never used them. When we took vacations to the lake or the beach, I kept a weather eye on the horizon for passing sails. I even, somewhere during this season, started a spiral-bound journal that I entitled *My Sea and Dream Book*. Several pages were dedicated to sketching my visions of ideal vessels—seat layouts, berths, galleys. Pencil and paper, at least, fell within my budget.

Having more fantasies than funds, I learned to make do with what was available to me. My first sailable vessel was not a sailboat at all, nor was it actually mine. The boat lived at a small cabin on Lake Burton in the north Georgia mountains. This was my family's vacation spot, one week every summer. As long as I can remember, an old aluminum canoe stayed propped against a pine tree in the little yard by the cabin. The unique thing about this canoe was its identity issues. Grumman Corporation engineers, perhaps inspired by the versatility required for their aircraft designs in World War II, showed an amazing capacity for creativity in the canoe world. Merely making a narrow vessel that two folks could paddle— that is, a canoe—was just too easy. The Grumman conversion canoe aimed to do everything any sort of boat could do. The result fell somewhere between impressive and comical.

Wes in Grumman
Lake Burton, Georgia

She was seventeen feet long, all aluminum, and at first glance, pretty normal. However, when I dragged the accessories from the cabin's storage closet, the Grumman began to morph. First, a specially made seat, designed to be clamped into the middle, made the canoe into a rowboat. Then, a peculiar apparatus that attached near the stern provided a motor mount for the small two-stroke Evinrude, which to my memory never actually cranked. Farther aft, right on the canoe's pointed end, was a hole for mounting an aluminum rudder. Why? Because, against all odds, this canoe could actually become a sailboat. By far its most impressive trick.

After the rudder came the bulky, white outriggers. Canoes are far too narrow of beam to handle the straining press of a sail, so the Grumman kit included long metal poles that clamped to the center of the canoe and attached, out over the water, to cylindrical Styrofoam pontoons. Traditionally, sailboats are known for their sleek beauty and curved majesty— what sailors call their "lines." Nothing in the nautical world is less sleek, less attractive, than big white tubes of Styrofoam hanging off the side of a floating Swiss Army Knife. However, appearances aside, the outriggers were functional and increased the stability of the canoe significantly.

Next came the mast, which fitted into a special slot at the canoe's bow, and from which flapped a large, unfaded, blue canvas. I was almost ready for the water now, but there was one final piece, without which the ship could not sail: centerboards. This critical component of sailing science is normally built, as the name implies, in the center of the vessel. However, a canoe, unlike a Rock Eagle Sunfish, has no slot through which a board can be lowered. Grumman's solution, predictably, was more clamps. An adjustable bar, tightened somewhere amid the tangle of outriggers and oarlocks and middle-seat clamps, held two wooden daggerboards, one on each side. They dropped into the water amidships.

The daggerboards were as attractive as any I've seen. They were sanded to a glassy smoothness and varnished to a mirror sheen. Set apart from the vessel itself, they looked fine, indeed. Even so, their aesthetic appeal was too weak to counter the look of the overall contraption, once all was finally pieced together. Imagine strapping a bedsheet to a gnarly piece of playground equipment flanked by huge pool noodles. That's a pretty close resemblance to my sailing canoe. Still, I loved that first boat, and I found it well suited for my weighty ballast of dreams. How many times Mom and Dad waved from the cabin's porch as my brother and I blew off into the looming backdrop of the Great Smokey Mountains. The cold clear water deep below us, the mystic Appalachians rising above. The swish of water sounding against our hull, the flap of wind in our sail.

I learned a great deal about sailing from that canoe. Being too ignorant and too lazy to actually read books on sailing, I did not know the terms for anything—not beyond the basic boat parts taught me at Rock Eagle. If someone had said "reach" or "run" to me in those days, I would have thought they meant "reach for a Coke out of the cooler" or "run because the game warden is coming and you're supposed to register sailboats over twelve feet."

Terminology aside, I gained a good feel for the various points of sail, and how to react to them. I learned that you'd better duck when the boom switches sides. I learned you get a gut sense for a boat's limits, particularly concerning listing in a crosswind. I learned that nearly every bad thing that occurs on a sailboat happens when running with the wind. I learned that when tacking (or "turning" as I would have called it), it's best to let the sheet out a bit and then reel it in incrementally as the boat gains speed—years later when I read this tip in a sailing book, I felt wonderfully validated.

While stocking up on skill, I never lightened up on vision. The dream, the underlying narrative or mythos, only grew. It was just a small lake in a light wind, a borrowed canoe with Styrofoam outriggers, but these were no hindrances to my story-laden mind. I remember sliding up out of the seat, sitting high on the V-shaped stern deck of the canoe, simply because it made me feel more like a proper sailorman. Ned Land would have sat there, sheet in one hand, tiller in the other, and Barbados over the horizon!

The Lake Burton Cabin

Grumman Under Full Sail

As the years passed, I continually dreamed of graduating beyond the Grumman. When I turned sixteen and obtained a driver's license, the dream became more possible. I had some money saved up from miscellaneous grass cutting jobs, and online boat listings gave me plenty to mull over. Vessels big and small scrolled across the computer screen, and each, to my indiscriminate eye, looked perfect, just perfect. As usual, I had more story than sense, and thus I felt less attraction for the small, manageable boats, and strong magnetism for the large and ship-like vessels. In hindsight, it would have been better and cheaper in the long run to have bought a simple Sunfish and been done with it. However, when there first appeared on the screen a type of sailboat called a pocket cruiser, I was smitten.

Until that moment, I did not know such a thing existed, but I saw right off that nothing could be more to the exact specifications of a sea-dreamer's fancy than these amazing sailboats. I had thought that only big boats—unaffordable yachts—had interiors. Here, though, was a trailerable craft with, miracle of miracles, windows looking out from a cabin. An honest to goodness belowdecks! Oh the fantasies that immediately populated my mind. Far off beaches with coconut palms, distant harbors, nights on deck with no land in sight and the stars overhead. Rolling waves, breaching whales, and berths before the mast lit by swinging lanterns. Images, fantasies, narratives—far weightier than practicality.

There was no talking sense to me at that point, especially when I discovered that the price of some of these pocket cruisers was notably lower than the price of small dinghies and daysailers. Three thousand dollars for a dinghy or one thousand for a pocket cruiser was, to me, an obvious choice. Thus, after a fearful, rainy drive through Atlanta traffic to Lake Lanier, I purchased my first vessel, a derelict 1972 Southcoast 22. Every dreamer's dream, rolling on two wheels, all for the low, low price of nine hundred and fifty dollars. I pulled that trailer and boat back to Cochran, the happiest kid in the state.

Though the boat was a wreck—full of water, cracked of fiberglass, rotten of wood—I experienced not a shred of buyer's remorse. In fact, after parking it in our yard and climbing all through the cabin, my dreams began to multiply. I particularly remember the dinette area, and how my mental pictures boiled over like so much chowder. I had visions of taking my family on sunset cruises, me working the sails on deck while they sat below sipping hot tea that had been steeped in the ship's galley. They would rest their mugs on cork-bottomed coasters to keep them from sliding on the little table. They would look out the oval shaped windows at the passing coastlines of Lake Blackshear or Lake Sinclair or Papeete.

Naturally, the truth punctured this vision when finally I got the boat out on the water. Sailing the Southcoast, as it turned out, was not a tea-sipping sort of affair. Perhaps on big, big boats one can reach that level of comfort, but I soon learned that twenty-two feet, massive as it then seemed to me, was a mere toy to the winds. The thought of holding a steaming mug while under sail was madness, truly a non-option. In fact, the idea of being belowdecks at all while underway, especially with an amateur captain at the helm, took more guts than most people cared to prove. If the boat flipped— and when aboard, to the inexperienced, she felt perpetually on the verge of capsizing—the unspoken preference was to be on deck, not trapped below. I knew none of this during the weeks spent doing my preliminary dry-land repairs. For hours on end I caulked and cleaned, fitted and fixed, and dreamed all the while, until finally it was time to seek the seas.

My maiden voyage was on Lake Juliette, near Macon, and I invited a full crew. Not one of us knew what we were doing. In the boat ramp's parking lot, we lugged the heavy mast up, up, up as my ship teetered on its trailer. That accomplished, we then backed thirty years of maritime history into the shallow Juliette waters. I'd bought a small Honda outboard to mount on the back, and we used it to motor away from the dock and into deeper waters. We then lowered the heavy iron keel using the hand winch built into the cabin. I had no owner's manual, no teacher, no guide, and therefore it was anybody's guess whether the keel was actually up or down or halfway in between. We went by feel, with it and everything else. All moves were by dead reckoning on that first trip.

Finally, we killed the engine and hoisted the mainsail. Spastically enough, I'm sure, but even amid our ineptitude, the old intoxicant of wind and sail, felt first at Rock Eagle, took my blood again. The charm, the deep magic, of raising sail, of seeing and hearing that flapping wildness billow out and snap to attention—it took hold of me afresh. Like a conjuring trick, the hull propelled forward. A beautiful wake churned behind the boat. She leaned. She lurched out. She came alive.

It was new and strange, and made all the more wondrous because it was mingled with a touch of fear. I was intimidated by this boat. Its size was not like anything I'd ever managed, and its geriatric status, supplemented by gallons of caulk, made for a thousand booby traps poised to spring or snap or leak or crack at any moment. I had no idea what to expect.

Fortunately, the Southcoast knew her business, even if I didn't. She found her own footing and plowed fearlessly forward. I'm sure she begrudged her handling by us landlubbery teenagers, but this nursing home escapee seemed happy enough to be on the water again. "Just leave me to it," she whispered, "and I'll behave."

In her confidence, I grew overconfident, soon calling out: "Hoist the jib! More speed, I say! Yaaargg!"

"I don't know," someone replied. "Looks a little dark over there."

"Nah, it's going around us. Hoist away!" It should be noted that, in those days, I maintained a perpetual and ineffective denial of any weather that threatened to spoil something I wanted to do. Storms were always "going around us."

"That looked like a flash of lightning," another pirate chimed in. A mutiny was brewing.

"It's just heat lightning," I asserted. In those days, it was always heat lightning, especially if at the given moment real lightning would have inconvenienced me.

The captain's word prevailed. The jib went up as the storm came down. It was a mistake. The wind swelled, and strange things began happening in hand and under foot. The tiller was getting stronger, suddenly arm wrestling against me. The boat itself became a shaky thing. It was speeding, speeding, faster and faster. It seemed charged, poised, ticking and bumping below us, something between a cougar ready to pounce and a submarine ready to dive. The wake behind our stern churned now like one behind a speedboat.

"Maybe we should get that jib down," I feebly suggested.

But it was too late. The first slap of a summer storm is its most violent moment, and this stormfront struck like an explosion. The Southcoast heeled hard over as the crew made an uncoordinated scramble to "Get that sail down!" and "Watch those rocks!" and "Crank up that Honda right now!"

The rain was driving down hard, making visibility minimal. We could see enough, though, to know that we were getting too near the bank, and that there really were rocks peeping up out of the water and laughing at us—their next meal. Also, and this is the part I remember most, I made a simple but costly rookie mistake, one that made the whole business worse than it needed to be.

It involved the mainsheet, which is the line that controls the mainsail. On the Rock Eagle Sunfish and the Lake Burton Grumman, the mainsheet was a straight rope held in the hand on one end and tied to the boom on the other. Simple and obvious. However, on the Southcoast, a direct line would have been too much pressure to handle, so the sheet ran through a series of pulleys to relieve the strain. This block-and-tackle system included pulleys on the port side, the stern side, and the boom. What I didn't know was the importance of tying a knot at the end of the mainsheet so that it couldn't escape the pulleys. I didn't see any reason to do this because the line was so long, a pile of rope at my feet, that it seemed impossible to ever reach the end of it. As it turned out, the length was only just enough. It looked like a great deal extra when close hauled, but if the mainsail was let out for a downwind run, all leftover line was spent reaching to the extended boom. When the blustering fury of our surprise storm snatched the sail and boom far out, it also snatched the mainsheet from my hand.

A dismal sight it was to see the end of that line slipping through the cam cleat, through the first pulley, then the next, and the next. "Oh! Oh! Oh!" I yelled, reaching wildly for the escaping rope, hoping to catch it before it blew overboard entirely, which would leave us at the mercy of an irrecoverable sail. All this in hard winds and flashing lightning and driving rain.

Mercifully, I grabbed it just before it made its last licking pass through the final pulley. It was still bad, but at least I had something. The problem now was that without the several looping passes of the block-and-tackle system, the full pressure of a wind-filled mainsail was transferred directly to my hand. Another problem, and more significant, was a science-of-sailing concept that I simply did not know at the time. The boom—that is, the pole that runs along the bottom of the mainsail—has a tendency to rise up when running downwind. The farther out the mainsheet stretches, the less able it is to enforce any sort of downward pressure on the boom.

To compensate for this, some vessels are fitted with a boom vang, which is essentially more rope and more pulleys, attached to the foot of the mast and to the boom. This can be cinched down to prevent any funny business when running downwind. Flying uncontrollably across Lake Juliette in the flooding rain, not one of us teenagers knew that boom vangs existed, much less that my Southcoast happened to not have one. And now that the mainsheet had slipped out of most of its pulleys, its ability to offer even a little downward pressure was further diminished. The boom, consequently, reared up and slapped down, reared up and slapped down, as the waves capped and the thunder clapped.

We were in danger, I now know, of something called an "accidental jibe," which is when the boom rises up to a point so high and volatile that it leaps to the other side. If on a downwind run the boom is stretched far out to starboard, it can get frisky and leap across to port. Since it makes this pass uninvited, the surprised crew has not reeled in the mainsheet as with an intentional jibe. In such a case, the sheet is fully extended as the sail snaps violently across the deck, with all that free line letting loose on the other side and the speeding sail going full bore when it snaps tight, in the process being unkind to line and equipment. Equally likely is that during the boom's overhead pass all that slack line will get tangled, and the sail, which is trying to reach full out for its run, will snatch too tight too soon. Suddenly the boat is close hauled, which can cause some nasty leaning. All of these were very real potentialities in that storm on Juliette, though all I knew then, vaguely yet absolutely, was that we were in a mess.

Two things, in the end, brought this episode to an anti-climactic close. One, our crack crew managed to wrestle the sails down. First the jib, which really didn't put up much of a fight, and then the mainsail, which being full of wind and let full out was a most uncooperative opponent. Secondly, the leading edge of the storm passed, and the dark cloud settled into a groove of easy rain.

Thus ended our shakedown run, and we, quite shaken ourselves, motored back to the dock and floated the big old beast onto her trailer. Soaking wet in the driver's seat of my Silverado, I pulled the ship home. Heading south on I-75, I reflected that weeks of preparation, gallons of caulk, and over a thousand dollars in expenses had bought me less than half an hour of actual, good sailing, and that the little taste I did get was speedily wrecked by a storm that, to this amateur, felt life-threatening.

Like so many boat owners before me, I asked myself the old question: *Was this really worth it?*

The answer came right on its heels, accompanied by a determined, almost intoxicated grin: *Absolutely.*

The Southcoast's Maiden Voyage
Lake Juliette, Georgia

I never returned to Lake Juliette with the Southcoast. Instead, I began to frequent the much larger Lake Sinclair, in Milledgeville, which was about an hour and a half from my house. Many successful Sinclair trips followed that rocky maiden voyage on Juliette. Over time, I learned much about sailing in general and the Southcoast in particular. I grew in comfort and confidence aboard my teenage yacht. So frequently did I make these weekend trips that I even rented a wet slip at a marina near the Sinclair dam. Hoisting the mast of a trailerable pocket cruiser is difficult work, but an uncovered slip allows the mast to be left up full time. Because of this new convenience, and because of the frequency of my trips, I began inviting a wider variety of friends on my weekend voyages. People knew, in those days, that I was always in need of a willing crew.

I therefore had several first timers with me on the infamous worst day. Every sailor has a story of his worst trip, and mine occurred one summer evening at Sinclair. We'd been sailing pleasantly for hours, and in the late afternoon were idly coming around a narrow passage near the dam, just passing by a large island known as Goat Island. All lake islands seem to be called that. As was my custom, I'd paid no attention to weather reports when planning this trip. I figured all was well. The wind was easy and the day had been calm. There was a bit of heat lightning beyond the trees, but nothing more.

I sat in the cockpit alone, with the mainsail locked into position and my hand lazily on the tiller. I reclined back against a life jacket, feeling comfortable and happy. A light drizzle started, but I thought nothing of it. It had been a hot day, and I liked the coolness of this little shower. Belowdecks, with the hatches closed, lounged all my friends, grilling stir fry on the Coleman stove and relaxing on the cushioned berths. I loved it. I felt like a true sailor—on the deck, manning the helm, holding the course, and transporting passengers. It felt authentic.

Oddly, the first convincing indication that something was wrong came through my seat. The Southcoast seemed to be coming alive, and I could feel it in the hull below me. Sailors get a sense for such things, especially when on a familiar boat. Something in the vibration and the bounce whispered trouble to me. I didn't like it.

Our speed was increasing rapidly. The flap of the sail grew louder, the rain harder. Accompanying this, and rising from nowhere, were waves. Salty sailors who've seen the seas will laugh at my mention of lake waves. Still, on a lake with long, straight stretches of water, the waves can be noteworthy, and my lack of experience magnified the size of these. They rolled behind us so that the boat felt the surge of surfing. The wind whipped, faster and faster, and I thought of my friends be-lowdecks. My vibe, in that moment, was that of a man leading a hiking party and just beginning to realize he might be lost but not willing to admit it. Then I made my two mistakes.

First, when an unexpected gust burst at me from astern, I somehow lost my grip on the mainsheet. It was an un-believable repeat of the Juliette voyage. Careless! I again hadn't tied a knot on the end of the line, and it slipped away, through one pulley, then another, then another. I grabbed at it desperately, but only managed to stop it on its last pass. Much like on Juliette, the sheet now was unrelieved by the block-and-tackle system, plus its downward exertion on the boom, so critical on a downwind run such as this, was greatly diminished. Not good.

Secondly, when a buddy from below slid open the hatch and stuck his head out, asking if I needed any help, I lied. He had felt the speed and pitch and roll from below and sensed that things were heating up. He just wanted to check, but like the lost hiker, I pretended all was well.

"No, no problem, I got it."

"Ok." He slipped back below and closed the hatch.

I should have accepted his help. Those below trusted that I knew what I was doing, and they were wrong.

That was when it hit—the great arm of the sky monster. It was violent. The wind and waves thus far had been only an opening act. Now the main event, with darkness, lightning, thunder, and howling wind. It was the work of a moment for the storm to snatch my mainsail from behind, lift the boom high above me, toss it across the deck in an "accidental jibe," and slam it down on the other side. Tragically, in the lift and toss, the already disheveled mainsheet got tangled into itself and did not release the boom beyond a close haul. In other words, the sail caught the full pressure of the wind and pressed it on the Southcoast at an angle that heeled us over—a stuck throttle on a sharp curve.

So mightily did the tangled sail grab the wind that the boat started coming about all on its own, without me being able to stop it. I physically could not handle the tiller, nor could I release the tangled sheet. That horrible, out of control feeling of a sailboat turning in a high wind, fully against my wishes—I'll never forget it. Within the flash of a lightning bolt we were cross wind and cross waves, and it laid us over. It is hard to capsize a heavy-keeled Southcoast 22, but I felt no such reassurance at the time. When we laid over, the deck now horribly perpendicular, I knew beyond doubt that the boat would keep rolling, right on over. It seemed obvious that this was it, *The Poseidon Adventure*, right here on the lake. I clung to the upper cockpit rail, hoping not to be pitched into the water, but my mind was, even in that moment, on the one obvious thing—my friends were all sealed in below.

If I'm sounding overdramatic, you must understand how little I knew back then. It wasn't until years later that I read an experienced sailor's comparison of a sailboat's cabin to a corked bottle on the waves. Whatever is inside the bottle may get tossed around, but the boat will stay buoyant for all that, bobbing on the surface. To my novice, teenage mind, I just knew they were all going to drown, nightmarishly trapped belowdecks.

This did not happen, though, because the Southcoast, when it laid over fully, continued to come about. It had a mind of its own now and pointed itself head up into the wind. Mercifully, this took the pressure off the sail and allowed the vessel to level out for a moment. The sail flapped in a wild, loud luff, and I used the opportunity to lower the outboard motor. In record time, I had the Honda dropped and cranked. Into the wind, into the wind, into the wind was all I could think as I revved the engine. The storm was an angry, howling thing still, and I did not want to be slapped broadside ever again. The sail, flapping straight over the cockpit, was still fully up, and I knew no way of getting it down without leaving the motor and walking up to the mast—an impossible maneuver in these circumstances.

No matter, for in that moment the main hatch slid open and a head popped out, a crewman clearly in full-on escape mode. He jumped up through the top hatch to about shoulder height, then, to complete the exit, yanked up the removable door that separated the cabin from the cockpit. I don't know if he threw it or the raging wind snatched it, but the door flew off into the lake and disappeared beneath the waves. He rushed on deck followed by two more well-shaken mateys. It must have been a horrible ride for them in that cabin when the boat rolled over. I felt terrible about it, but it was too early for apologies.

"Get the sail down!" I called while keeping one hand death-gripped to the outboard and the other to the tiller. "We've got to get that sail down!"

In the rain and wind and waves, they climbed over the cabin to the bow and started untying lines. The jib came down easily, but the real enemy was the mainsail. I could not breathe until that dragon was back in its cave. They undid the mainsail halyard and yanked down on the canvas. It moved about a foot, then stopped. It should have fallen smoothly toward the deck. They yanked again, a good heave ho, then called back to me, "It's stuck!"

Indeed, it was, very stuck. I figured the line must have jumped off the pulleys that crown the top of the mast, twenty-plus feet in the air and well out of reach. The harder they pulled on the sail—and no doubt they were tugging hard —the deeper the line wedged into the gap beside the pulleys. I saw no way to get the mainsail down, and the storm was still full force.

Once again, a real sailor would have known what to do. In fact, the answer had been within my reach the whole time. At the aft end of the boom, which was flopping around my head, was a release line for just such occasions. A simple unwrapping from that cleat and the mainsail would have been tamed, folded not down as with a typical lowering, but forward toward the mast in a more emergencies-only type release.

But I didn't know. So instead, the intrepid crew proceeded to roll the sail any which way they could, grabbing at excess canvas and yanking, twisting, tying, wrapping. Though not a textbook lowering by any standards, it worked. The sail's surface decreased drastically and converted our wind-ship into a far safer motorboat. We were still in the storm, but we were out of the woods. Everyone gathered with me in the cockpit. We huddled against the rain as the Honda hummed on.

"Sorry about your door," my friend said.

"Forget it. Sorry I almost killed us," I said.

"It won't happen again."

Sitting there, I could see through the doorless passage into the cabin. It was a total wreck. Towels, cushions, life jackets, plates, plasticware, a frying pan, and all the things I normally kept stowed neatly in their places, were tossed about like clothes in a dryer. On top of it all was leftover stir fry, flung from the pan that had been cooling on the stove.

We were as shaken as the cabin, and with the howling storm and the growing darkness, no one wanted to fight our way back to the marina. We therefore decided to head straight for the nearest dock and tie off. This we did, feeling much better the moment dry land was beneath our feet. We walked across the yard of who-knew-whose house and knocked on the stranger's door. We must have looked honest, or pitiable, or both, because the nice fellow, after hearing our tale of woe, agreed to give us a ride in his station wagon. He drove us several miles to the marina and dropped us at our vehicles. Then we, the soaking survivors, loaded up and drove home.

When I got back to Cochran, I announced to my parents that I would be selling the boat. I meant it, too, for in truth the experience had shaken me up. Even so, there was still the problem of retrieval. The Southcoast was tied to some stranger's dock somewhere on Lake Sinclair. The next day I asked a different buddy of mine—somehow the ones from the storm were not answering their phones—if he would come along and help me find my boat. He agreed, and off we went.

Once in Milledgeville, I didn't really know where to go. We crossed 441 at the big intersection, wove through some side streets, turned at a small wooden church, and found ourselves in a labyrinthine neighborhood where all looked alike. The fact is, I had not paid much attention to what turns the man had made on our ride in the station wagon in the rainy darkness. Now in the broad daylight, I recognized nothing. Also, I thought we would be able to see the water from the road, in which case we could just drive around until we saw my boat, but no such luck. The large houses and wide yards and full-grown trees kept the lake out of view. We eventually had to just guess.

I parked the truck on a curb, and we nervously walked across a well-manicured lawn to knock on the front door of a fine looking house. We simply wanted permission to walk around back and look for our boat at the lake's edge. Admittedly, this story felt exactly like something a criminal might say, and I knew it.

We stood at the door and knocked the fancy golden knocker.

Footsteps echoed inside for a moment, then the door swung open. A foreign man looked right at us and, I kid you not, went immediately into a passionate explanation, nearly frantic, in a heavy accent: "Oh, we got the rent money. We get the rent money. We have the rent money. You not worry. The rent money coming!"

It was an odd thing, and I didn't exactly know what was happening or how to respond. I suppose he thought me and my friend were two goons sent by the landlord to "rough him up" until he paid. Whatever the case, we had a bit of a time getting the fellow to stop and understand that we didn't know anything about him or his overdue rent, but that we simply wanted to walk around to his backyard and look for our boat. He was so happy to find out we were not collectors that he agreed.

With that peculiar bar crossed, we walked around back and saw the old Southcoast just a few houses down, faithfully floating at the stranger's dock. I crossed some lawns, climbed aboard, and motored off around Goat Island and back to the marina. My friend drove the truck around and met me at the landing. We loaded up the boat and hit the road. On the ride to Cochran, after a good laugh about our encounter with the tenant, I had plenty of time to reflect. Somewhere along boring old 441, I changed my mind about selling the boat. Sailors, especially the story-filled dreamer type, have amazingly short memories about such things. There's always the next trip, and the next trip will be better.

The Southcoast, unsold and re-caulked, eventually returned to Lake Sinclair. There were some lesser outings between, taken on the shallow waters of Lake Blackshear, nearer to my house, but it was this fresh return to Sinclair that brought about the boat's best trip. I had a full crew for this one. They were all first timers, repeat customers proving rare. We launched at my usual marina and motored out into the open lake.

"Alright," I said, "here goes." I killed the motor and climbed into the cabin to crank down the keel winch. This was normally a tame procedure. Somehow, though, the heavy iron keel broke loose and fell freely down, down, down. It whammed unkindly into its lowered position, busting a hole in its fiberglass housing near the bow. Thankfully, the puncture was above the waterline. The keel, though, was now detached from the winch and therefore stuck in the lowered position.

"What was that?" someone asked.

"We're good," I said, clambering out of the cabin with a socket wrench in hand—because that's a scene boat guests want to see. "I think the keel came loose, but I was planning on fixing it anyway"—because that's a line boat guests want to hear. It was true, though. Naturally, I had not expected the keel to break loose like that, but I had somewhat expected problems with it, sooner or later. The fact was that the rusty clamps on the keel cable had come loose once before when I ran aground on a Lake Blackshear trip, and I had only been able to manage a spit-and-glue repair job since then. I knew it would not hold forever, though I didn't advertise this to potential crewmates. Since I now had these newbies shanghaied, there was no harm in coming clean. Still, it must have been an uneasy sight watching their captain, socket wrench in one hand and cable clamp in the other, jump overboard.

I had done a similar repair the day the cable first broke at Blackshear. For that one, my brother and I had pulled the boat into a shallow cove so that one of us could stand on the muddy bottom and push up on the heavy hunk of iron, while the other stood in the cockpit and pulled on a rope we had run through the self-bilge tube and tied to the keel. I learned then that I did not like, did not like at all, working underwater. I kept thinking how easy it would be for that keel to fall on me, pinning me to the soft bottom forever.

Now on Lake Sinclair, I felt that same distaste for being under a boat without an oxygen tank. Here, though, we were in deep water. The bottom was who-knew-how-far below. There was no chance of getting pinned to the mud, but the murky black emptiness that loomed beneath my feet created its own sort of uneasiness. Also, I faced the natural problem of my body's buoyancy. I had to take a deep breath before diving under the boat, but my chest full of air kept floating me up against the underside of the hull. I didn't like this.

It had to be done, though, so down I went. In the murk, I surveyed the situation. Yes, there was the loose cable. Up for air. Down again, grabbing the cable and wrapping it around the keel. Up for air. Down again to attempt the cable clamp. Up and down and up and down, no doubt to the entertainment and confusion of the crewmen on deck. I remember coming up once, setting my tools on the foothold by the starboard window, and hanging there to catch my breath.

"I'm sorry about this, guys," I said. "I know this isn't fun."

They were good sports. "Hey, we understand. You gotta keep it working. No problem."

What they said after I dived down again, well, who knows.

In the end, though, I managed to get the keel cable tightly wrapped and securely clamped. Better still, I didn't drown. Back on deck, I was now ready for some sailing. And sail we did! All over the lake we went that day. We sailed to the dam, then back again. We sailed around the island where I'd lost my door. We sailed up the lake, on the long, straight stretch that is the main body of Sinclair. When the wind cooperated, we had both sails going. When the tacking back and forth became too much work, or impractical in the narrows, we lowered the sails and cranked the motor. In the afternoon, a little squall blew through, with that typical high-wind slap of a storm's front edge. We shot right through it, sails up, fearless. This was nothing compared to what I'd seen last time. The boat leaned into the whipping wind, the crew and I leaning with it, laughing. In that quick storm, we tasted the peculiar pride boaters feel when all the other lake-goers are speeding to the docks for cover while your own boat rides fearlessly outward.

Before the day ended, we had sailed as far as the Highway 441 bridge. There was a small dockside store there, and I felt like a true old salt when we cruised into a slip, deployed crewmen to tether bow and stern lines, and went in to buy honeybuns—to prevent scurvy. I was no longer an untrained teenager blundering around a muddy lake on his cheap, crack-hulled craft. I was on the high seas. I was Nemo and Farragut, Smollett and John Silver. The Southcoast was a well-trimmed schooner, rum running and island charting and honey bun smuggling. Yaaargg.

The voyage became better still at night. Intoxicated by the watery sunset and mysticism that is always twilight, I made a bold suggestion to the crew: "I want to spend the night." Under other circumstances, they probably would have replied, "Well, have fun!" But because we had carpooled to the lake, a certain degree of diplomacy was required on their part. After all, among our crew of four, only two people had the keys to the vehicles, and one of them was a Quixotic captain who suddenly wanted to anchor off the Cape of Good Stories and spend the night aboard ship, without pillows or sleeping bags or breakfast.

The announcement ran through everyone's thoughts, along, I'm sure, with machinations of mutiny. Some mentioned that they had church tomorrow, and some that they needed their parents' permission. The conversation rippled around like this a bit, but the tidal shift came when the other driver said he thought it was a good idea. With him willing, the trap was set. In truth, I don't think I was piratical enough to actually keep anyone in Milledgeville if they—or more importantly, their parents—insisted they come home. Still, I badly wanted this night on the lake, and I silently considered the efficacy of coercion versus convincing. Of "We've got the car keys!" versus "Don't you *want* to stay?"

With both vehicle owners all set to stay, a third crewman admitted his willingness, if not eagerness, to give it a try, so the vote settled at three against one. The final fellow held out firmly. As a way to buy more time to press my case, I suggested we dock the boat and drive into town to get some food.

This we did, and after eating, I stalled further by taking us to the Milledgeville Walmart. I even made so bold as to put some camping rations in my buggy—water and Cokes and frozen stir fry. On a whim, I also picked up a CD of

Jimmy Buffett's greatest hits album, *Songs You Know by Heart.* This proved a powerful, if unwitting, move. On the ride from Walmart back to the lake, we listened to Buffett. My best arguments for staying were not one-hundredth as effective as this little yellow album. The first three songs had him weakening, but it was "Son of a Son of a Sailor" that scaled the final wall. And when track five, "A Pirate Looks at Forty," rolled out of the speakers, the takeover was complete. He slapped the dashboard with both hands, looked at me, and said, "Let's stay!"

Story did that. The visions painted by the narrative poetry of Jimmy Buffett took over the heart, even after all my arguments had failed to win the mind. To think that stories are a mere pastime, and that the real business of living, surviving, and thriving happens elsewhere, is to misunderstand humans entirely. Stories affect waking reality. Yes, storytellers run the country.

The darkening night found our swashbuckling crew motoring out into our own Caribbean Sea, seeking anchorage and adventure. I wanted to be as far from land as possible, like Nemo. Instead of choosing a spot tucked away in some cove, which would have been safe and logical, we instead anchored right out in the middle of the lake. This was stupid, dangerous, and entirely my fault, but my storied mind would settle for nothing less than the lake's "Point Nemo."

Worse still, the Southcoast's built-in nav lights did not work, so we instead attached a kerosene lantern to the jib halyard and ran it up the shroud. Or as I would have said back then: *We hooked it to that rope and ran it up that wire.* Nomenclature aside, the little flame gave only a meager light and served us poorly in the safety department, though it worked well in the story-dream category. It looked nautical. The lantern glow on deck, the starlit sky above, the rocking back and forth on gentle waves, the whole universe reflected below us, it all felt right. We were transported.

One crewman got sleepy before the rest of us, and he was already in bed when we began dealing with the food we'd bought for our nighttime snack. He was in the double berth at the bow, and this put his head right next to the galley, so to avoid waking him up or setting his hair on fire, we moved the stove to the bow deck and huddled as best we could around the blue propane glow. One of the crewmen took charge as lead chef. He placed a metal skillet on the grating and let it heat up, then dumped the frozen contents of the bagged Asian cuisine into the pan. As the ice flakes melted off, the green beans and peas and chicken chunks let up a steam that danced nicely into our noses.

With only a few burnt fingertips, we managed to get the finished stir fry distributed onto the Walmart paper plates. We ate it with plastic forks, washing it down with tepid Cokes. We then spread out around the deck—on the bow, in the cockpit, by the mast—and reclined with our bellies full and our adventure real. We were, in that moment, Sons of Sailors. At that teenage season of life, having only recently acquired the right to drive a car, here we were living before the mast.

Much later, after the food settled and the conversation fizzled, we had to say goodnight to the sky full of stars. We crawled into the cabin and slid the hatch shut behind us. Quietly, so as not to wake the sleeping crewman, we shuffled around to our chosen berths. I took the best bed for myself, I'm ashamed to admit. I'm sure I justified it back then, thinking *I'm the captain* and *I paid for this boat* and so forth, but there was no excuse for it. It was my idea to spend the night, and I should have given them the best beds. I didn't, though, and there's no rewriting that. The starboard berth became Captain's Quarters, and the others had to make do elsewhere.

We spent a cold, cramped night blanket-less on the lake. Despite all that, I was in my element. The quiet lapping of the water beside me, the mystical depths of the murky lake below. We heard fishermen motoring around until the wee hours, their whining outboards speeding past us, reminding me how downright stupid it was to anchor in the middle with inadequate lighting. Several times, some exceptionally near passes woke us, and the waves rocked us sharply. We couldn't hear what these fishermen were saying, but I'm sure it was something like, "Is that a…YES! TURN!" This followed by some unprintables.

Mercifully, no one hit us. Morning arrived safely, and in the manner of all uncomfortable campers, we rose early, happy to get the heck out of bed. The sunrise was cool and silent, the water a sheet of glass. A painted vessel on a frozen lake. I fired up the dew-drenched Honda, and the Southcoast slit like a blade through the smooth water, toward the marina, toward the mainland. We'd survived the night, and Captain Nemo, at least, had an amazing time. As for the others, well, I don't remember any ever asking to do it again. Perhaps they just needed a little yellow CD by Jimmy Buffett, or a little green paperback by Jules Verne.

Redwall & Red Fern

Life wasn't all nautical, and *20,000 Leagues* was only one story among many. I carried them all in my heart, some at the forefront and others in the background. One that took over in elementary school was a fantasy novel entitled *Redwall*, by Brian Jacques. I found it in the school library one day and dove in immediately, not knowing a thing about it. I visited Redwall Abbey and Mossflower Woods for the first time that day, meeting Matthias and all the other critters and characters. I was absorbed into the story's world, wholly immersed.

Like most stories in my life, this fiction soon crossed the threshold into the waking world. In the novel, two of the abbey mice, Matthias and Methuselah, follow a series of ancient riddles to discover a secret passage hidden below the middle step on a flight of stairs. I loved this scene. My heart began to yearn for secret passageways. My eyes scanned walls and corners, nooks and crannies, to see if a hidden door might be lurking about, some secret room of school or house or church—especially church—accessed only by pulling a candlestick or pushing a discolored stone. I developed a peculiar grudge against the generations who lived before me, for their selfish shortsightedness in not leaving a treasure or a map, a clue or a riddle, a door or a passage for the coming generations.

This grudge then morphed into a project: I would leave something for those who came after me. I would not neglect this obvious duty. Of course, I couldn't install an actual secret passage in our house, but I could hide something and draw a map. I decided on a time capsule, and straightaway began preparing mine.

I knew I needed something that would not deteriorate while buried in the damp ground, and also something water-tight, so I decided to use a glass jar. I went to the refrigerator in our kitchen and looked for the emptiest one—no sense in wasting food. The best candidate was a glass container of Pace Picante Sauce. It was nearly empty, and as an added bonus, it was uniquely shaped. Pace jars narrow down in the middle, like an hourglass. This was fitting.

A more practical advantage was the jar's metal lid, which would aid any future searchers armed with metal detectors—and presumably everyone in the year 2097 would have metal detectors in their wristwatches. Yes, I was thinking like a true archaeologist. A final Pace advantage was that I liked salsa a great deal, and therefore could dispose of its remaining contents more pleasurably than, say, a jar of olives. I poured the salsa into a bowl, pulled a bag of tortilla chips from the cabinet, and got to work. Archeology wasn't a bad gig. Then, I washed the now-empty jar in the kitchen sink and dried it thoroughly, ready to face the dilemma of what to put in-side. I did not have much that was actually valuable, and the things I did have were either too big to fit in the jar or too likely to get me in trouble if my parents found out I'd buried them in the yard. I soon realized, however, that inexpensive contents were just as good, because it was the passage of time that would ultimately instill the value. Anything is awesome if dug up 100 years later.

I dropped a few coins into the jar. Mostly just regular currency, quarters and dimes and such, but also a few fifty-cent pieces and some foreign coins I'd collected. I figured futuristic humans would be interested to see what sort of money we used in the 1990s. I also pulled a few pages from *The Macon Telegraph*, rolled them tightly, and shoved them into the jar. I put in other things besides, but I forget what they were.

The next decision was where to bury it. We lived in a quiet neighborhood in town, which at first didn't seem the right place for a time capsule. I wanted a wilderness, like in *Redwall*. At least our yard was larger than a typical town lot, and at the back of it was a vacant property grown with trees—it was the imaginative forest of my childhood. The more I considered it, the more I liked it. This would be the perfect spot.

That settled, I proceeded with the mapmaking. Matthias had clues to lead him to his secret staircase, and my future time-capsule discoverer would have more fun if he had a map. As I selected my precise burial spot, I marked distances from things that I figured would stand the test of time. The barn in our backyard, for instance, felt permanent, so I paced from there. Also, the larger trees in the woods seemed the very emblems of longevity, so I used them as marking points for the final dig site. Fifty paces here, ten paces there, and so on. I jotted down all these notes carefully.

Then, with the specific location triangulated, I got a

shovel from the barn and took to digging. I envisioned my-self eventually standing in a deep hole, deeper than I was tall, and tossing dirt over my head, up to the surface. The reality proved less dramatic. The roots, roots, roots made digging almost impossible for my little ten-year-old self. I chopped more than I dug. After cutting a gnarled ball of roots, I'd scrape out what dirt I could and chop some more. I labored on, only to find after much sweat that the hole was barely over the depth of the shovel's head. This was intolerable. I knew the capsule needed to be buried deep if it was to stand the test of time—I didn't want a rainstorm or a nosey dog to unearth my treasure. I pressed on, digging and chopping, digging and chopping.

Finally, I put the sauce jar with its strange contents into the rooty hole and covered it up with the soft black dirt. I packed it down with shovel slaps and shoe stomps, and ended by sprinkling a layer of leaves to make things look natural. The deed done, I put the shovel away, wiped my hands on my pants, and went inside to draw the final draft of the map.

I sat at the little wooden desk in my upstairs bedroom, the same one from the *Frankenstein* experiment, and pulled out my private journal. I kept a regular journal in those days—thanks to Professor Aronnax, of course—and it seemed the perfect place for the first official map to my time capsule. I sketched lines and noted key landmarks. I paused, ran outside to remeasure a few critical distances, and came back to jot them down. Everything was marked in units of paces, because that felt more primitive, though they would only be accurate if the reader also happened to be a short legged ten-year-old.

I put a date at the top of the page. The year, I remember distinctly, was 1997. I closed the journal, satisfied.

Then I began to think that this wasn't enough. My journal was a private thing, and I wanted the map to be findable by the future residents of our house. It seemed unfair to hide something so completely that no one would ever discover it. Plus, I wanted this future someone to have the Matthias-like experience of following clues. That was the original inspiration, after all. In the end, I decided to draw another map and hide it somewhere in the house.

I got a piece of notebook paper out of my Trapper Keeper and went back to my desk to work. Propping my journal open, I sketched a modified copy of the original map, clues included. That done, I now had to decide where to hide it. Nothing easy, of course, but not impossible either. There was a balance to treasure hiding, I realized, and this led to some trial-and-error work. I first stuck the new map behind some books. No good. Then, in some books. No again. Under a rug. Of course not. On and on until, finally, a serious candidate appeared in the shape of our brick chimney. I liked the solidity of it, the feeling of permanence. I'd often noticed on rides out in the country the lone chimneys standing like monuments where a house once stood. I folded the paper into a square and then stuffed it into the tiny crack between the chimney and the adjoining wall in our kitchen. To give the future discoverers a sporting chance, I left a tiny corner of the paper peeping out.

I felt satisfied as I walked away, but soon the doubts whispered in. This spot was too easy, too exposed. Likely it would be found within a decade, a year, a week. Someone in my own family would spot it and find it. The map and treasure would be unearthed while we still lived here, and that was not the dream. In *Redwall*, Martin the Warrior was dead and gone by the time Matthias and Methuselah followed the ancient riddles.

That evening, I sat down to an uneasy supper with the family. We ate in the kitchen, and the table was right next to the chimney. I kept an eye on their faces. Did they suspect? Would they spot it? I pictured the scene: "Pass the green beans—hey, what's that?" This was intolerable.

As soon as the meal was over and everyone drifted on to other things, I used the tip of a pencil to grab the map's corner and pull it from its crevice. This spot was no good. The next day I tried a new place, and it was a classic moment of overcompensation. The chimney was certainly too easy, but the final resting place of this map was too impossible. What's done is done, though. I hid it there and left it for good. That house has long since been sold, and I imagine the map has not moved from its hiding spot. And no, I'm not telling where that is.

The real difficulty about this whole business was my impatient mind. A time capsule is only fascinating if there is a passage of time. Having buried my own, I now learned the glacial slowness of clocks and calendars. After only a few days, I was itching to dig the jar up. I repeatedly looked back in my journal to ascertain the exact date, gauging if it was okay to go ahead and dig. Still the same year, same month, same week! In order to survive this, I needed a new perspective. There was only one way to stand up under the weight of such anticipation—I had to just forget about it. Forget I'd buried anything. Forget I'd drawn a map. Forget it, forget it, forget it. Time moves faster when you don't look at it.

But it is a hard thing to remember to forget something, to think about what not to think about. I struggled on, until eventually my mercurial nature came to the rescue. With the reading of another book and watching of another movie, my thoughts began to follow other scents. I soon forgot what I was supposed to forget, and that was the unconscious victory.

Only once did the subject again come up during those childhood days in that house, and it was in the most *Redwall* of fashions. My dad, at some point or other, did an extensive remodel of our flooring. The whole house, for my whole life, had been covered with thick blue carpet, accompanied by blue molding, blue baseboards, blue trim, blue wallpaper, and, I'm not kidding, blue doors. Affectionately, we called our home "The Smurf House." We all knew it looked ridiculous. Dad's solution for breaking up this monotone palette was to change the flooring—out with the blue carpet, in with the brown wood.

I was only passingly interested in this project until one day when Dad's replacing of a squeaky subfloor board revealed a sort of hidden room. That got my attention. An adult would call it merely a nook or space, one of those unavoidable necessities of architecture, but to my storied mind it was a secret passage, a hidden vault, a lost chamber. Our house, which had always disappointed me with its unmoving bookcases and not-secret-lever candlesticks had finally come through! This was just like Matthias and Methuselah's discovery.

Right away I knew I had to capitalize on this. It was an

opportunity not likely to present itself again. I set to work gathering a few "treasures" and making a neat pile of them in the secret vault. The main item I remember was a book—included because I liked the idea of future searchers finding an ancient text with dusty covers and yellowed pages. That felt right.

I also created and included a new copy of the time capsule map. I then went and retrieved the other hidden map, amending it to include instructions on how to find the secret room beneath the subfloor. I was determined that any future discoverer who found one would be able to find all. I'm surprised my silly self didn't go dig up the time capsule and add a map on how to find the hidden maps, but to my credit I never went back to the Pace jar.

Wes in Blue House
Just a few feet from a hidden map.

As far as I know, all three secrets are hidden right where I left them. The jar in the ground, the first map in its place, and the new map in the vault beneath the floor. I can only hope that one day some kid, after reading a tale like *Redwall* with hidden riddles and tangled clues and secret stairs, will let his imagination carry him on a pretend treasure hunt. He'll be envisioning himself as Matthias, searching around the Abbey for the ancient and lost. It will be just a game, of course. Nothing there to actually find. Just having fun with the make-believe. And then: What's this? A bit of paper? It looks old. It's rather brittle. It looks like a...oh my!

I, myself, never had such a lucky moment (more's the pity), but before *Redwall* left my life, it did bring a treasure of a different sort to me. It wasn't buried or hidden, but it was special and wonderful. At the beginning of Book II, readers encounter an uncommunicative baby red squirrel named Silent Sam. His trademark, besides never talking, is that he constantly sucks his paw. I remember him across the years, how he befriended me from the pages of the book. I wanted so badly to have such a squirrel—to let him scurry around my bedroom, to make him a little nest-bed in a dresser drawer, to pet him and hold him and hug him.

It was an odd thing to care about, I suppose, but there it was. I even began reading up on squirrels. I found one writer who shared how he sat still in his yard, daily, until the squirrels acclimated to him and came near enough to eat out of his hand. I tried that, sitting under a big pine tree in the backyard of our blue house, but I was never able to hold still long enough to meet success. I was a wiggly child, high on dreams but short on resolve. The squirrels kept their distance from this nut.

I therefore decided to try a squirrel trap. I don't know where I got it, but most probably I begged my parents, and they either bought it or borrowed it from somewhere. As with most of my childhood projects, my sudden enthusiasm for this or that hobby—sailboat today, squirrel trap tomorrow—was a perpetual mystery to others. I knew the story behind each pursuit, but that was a hard thing for others to see.

I set my trap by the woods at the back of our yard. It was a wire-cage contraption, about the size of a shoebox, and had two spring-loaded doors hinged on each end, with a trigger mechanism in the middle. If rigged properly, the lightest touch would release the doors, snapping them shut. This I learned when I tried adding the dry corn that I was using as bait. Just a few pellets on the trigger and *clap!* down on my arm. Thankfully, it was not a sharp-toothed sort of trap, so it did no more harm than a jack-in-the-box jump scare. I tried again, more carefully, and finally got the corn on the trigger without incident. I also sprinkled some kernels around the outside, to lure the critters in. The game was on.

I stared out our kitchen window, waiting. From there I could see if the trap's doors were up and loaded, or snapped down and locked. The latter was the sight I anxiously desired, knowing it meant I had a catch. Nothing happened, and so I went off to play something else, resolving to check the trap periodically. For the rest of that day, nothing. Then the next and the next and the next, still nothing. But one evening, after visiting my grandparents, we pulled into our driveway, and I saw in the glow of the headlights that the doors of the cage were down. I jumped out of our van and ran to the woods to meet my prize. Sure enough, it was a squirrel. Not a red squirrel like Silent Sam, but a beautiful, fluffy-tailed gray. I carried the cage back toward the house as the poor animal went wild inside.

This was when I learned that my toothless trap did, after all, hurt its captive, or rather it allowed the animal to hurt himself. His snout was bloody from running into the cage's wires for however long he had been in there. That made me sad. After watching him in the cage for a while, and showing him off to the family, I eventually felt he needed to be set free.

He was getting hurt. Plus, he wasn't red like Sam, so I needed the trap vacant so I could try again. In a gesture toward scientific inquiry—these were also my *Frankenstein* days—I marked him on the belly with a single squirt of golden spray paint before turning him loose in the backyard.

I kept this trapper's game up for weeks, catching a good many squirrels, staring at them for a bit, and then setting them free. I liked them all, and badly wanted one, just one, to be sociable, to ride on my shoulder, to take a name and come when I called it. But none lived up to the dream. Even when I caught a repeat customer, the squirrel with the golden paint, he still had not warmed up to me. Furthermore, all of my catches were gray, which was a continual disappointment to my storied mind.

In truth, I didn't even know if red squirrels lived in Georgia like they did in the Mossflower Woods of *Redwall*. Still, I trapped on, and eventually, against all odds, I caught a beautiful little squirrel with reddish hair. Was it just a gray squirrel with a distant redheaded ancestor? Or one whose pigment had been affected by the sun? I didn't know, nor did I much care. This, finally, was my Silent Sam.

Naturally, he didn't suck his paw—we'd have to work on that—but he did avoid speech in a very Sam-like way. I counted that a good start and decided I could, with some patience, train him as a pet. I proposed to my parents that we bring him into the house. Now ours was not an animal friendly interior. We had one dog at the time, a gigantic golden retriever, and he never crossed the threshold indoors. Somehow, though, I talked my parents into it with this squirrel, and I moved him, still in the trap, to the kitchen, right by the chimney that had once held my map. I gave him water and food, both of which he spilled. I tried to pet him through the bars, always with him cowering away. Still, I felt good about the arrangement and determined to keep trying. The only thing that bothered me was his scuffed nose, bloodied from hitting the bars in his attempts to escape. I knew I wouldn't want this to happen to the real Sam, and therefore I decided that he needed more room, even if just a little more.

I went out to our shed and found an old milk crate. Its metal wire mesh looked similar to the squirrel trap. The spacing between the bars was a bit wider, but still too small, I figured, for a squirrel to fit through. Only two holes, the crate's handles, seemed large enough to be trouble, so I taped over one and used the other as his entryway. My idea was that if I connected the two cages, Sam could pass freely from the crate to the cage and back again, thus doubling his square footage. I placed the milk crate next to Sam's cage, applied duct tape in all the necessary places, and opened one of the trap's spring-loaded doors. Out shot that little red squirrel like something from a Ray Stevens song, straight through the milk crate, and freely into the kitchen. Oh no! I had grossly underestimated the ability of these critters to get skinny. The milk crate's bars didn't even slow him down.

Around the kitchen he ran, and then onto the sill of the big window where he promptly knocked over a small pine tree seedling I was growing for a school project. Dirt spilled all over the floor. He scurried onto my mom's desk, disrupting papers, and then up the chimney side and onto the shelving above the desk. There he finally took cover under a phone book and squatted perfectly still. I gave my parents the apologetic *oops* face. To their credit, they took it quite well. The problem remained, though: how to get the squirrel out of the house? Squirrels have teeth, and nobody wanted to grab this frightened, cornered animal.

He sat there, frozen and staring. We stared back. Eventually, Dad got the broom and gave him some encouragement. It was quite a commotion.

"He's going."

"Quick, head him off there!"

"Close that door!"

"Open that one!"

"There you go."

"No not that way, this way."

And on it went until, finally, the frightened little fellow caught sight of the sunlight out the open kitchen door and shot into the garage, to the yard, free. Away he went forever, chittering a happy goodbye.

"Goodbye, Sam. I'll miss you."

As time passed, I drifted away from *Redwall* and through sundry other stories, until in my mid-teens a new narrative again sent me to the world of animals. This time the vibe was less fantastical and more down to Earth. It all began with *Where the Red Fern Grows*, that wonderful Ozark story by Wilson Rawls. I actually saw it rather than read it, meeting Billy Coleman and his two redbone hounds through the 1974 film adaptation, but whether experienced through book or movie, *Where the Red Fern Grows* is one of the most moving stories ever told.

The ache Billy feels for want of something he can't have,

and then the gutsy determination he employs to work, work, work for it—this is a timeless ideal, the property of all humanity. Many a man, myself included, has gained grit from having known Rawls's story. It is by grit that Billy earns the money to buy the dogs. It is grit that lends him the strength to walk all the way to Tahlequah, barefoot, to get them. And it is grit that gives him the resolve to hatchet an impossibly huge sycamore tree on his first hunt. Billy develops a bond with his redbones, Dan and Ann, that is nearly Edenic. But as with Eden, there is a snake in the garden. In the story, Billy learns about bullies, death, and the stale crust of giving up. Because of a tragic accident on a wager-induced coon hunt, he vows to never hunt again. Then comes an upswing of redemption and hope, followed by a valley of loss and decision, all finally culminating in one of the most poetic endings in all of storytelling, which I dare not spoil.

Everything about this story worked for me and in me during my transitional adolescent years. I came to long for the woods, and I wanted a dog with me. I asked my parents and found them a bit less enthusiastic about the idea of a new pet. However, the problem soon solved itself when a little stray puppy, brown with a black snout, unwittingly wandered into my life at just the time I was dreaming of Ozark adventures. He took up residence at an old, run-down farmhouse my parents owned, out in the rural Bleckley County countryside. We adopted him, named him Bullet, and moved him to our blue house in town. He became my Dan and Ann, my friend for adventures in the forests.

Fittingly, one of my first outings with Bullet happened not in flatland Bleckley County, but in the north Georgia mountains—my own Ozarks. We took our annual trip to the cabin at Lake Burton, the same cabin with the Grumman sailboat, and this time Bullet went with us. I was thrilled. There was a cluster of mountains right behind the cabin, and this became mine and Bullet's playground. In true Billy Coleman fashion, I went barefoot. My soles were tough in those days. I remember one day that week, as I chased Bullet up the mountain, I stepped on a busted glass bottle and hardly felt a thing. It neither cut me nor hurt me. I just kept on running.

The more time I spent there, the more I learned about the difference between mountain country and flat country. For one thing, flatness was easier to navigate, directionally. Back home I could usually walk straight into the woods and then turn around and walk straight out. Not so in the mountains, where you don't go straight up and in, but round and round. I became frequently disoriented because everywhere I turned led to a cliff or bank or gully that required me to turn again. I would be working around one mountain, around and up like a corkscrew, when that mountain would mesh into another mountain, and I'd have to start working around the new one. Then that one would mesh again, and again, until I lost track of which was which. I was not in a forest of this mountain here and that mountain there, but rather in a boiling collision of all mountains together, and they all looked the same. At each collision point, there would be a valley, often with a creek, but each valley and each creek looked just like the one before. The whole business was confusing.

Another peculiarity that surprised me was my inability to reach the top of the mountains behind the cabin. It wasn't for lack of trying. I would work my way up, up, and around,

Sometimes I would even try a straight-on frontal attack, which in places got quite steep, even too steep for Bullet. However, whether ascending this way or that, all I found at any potential peak was another boiling landmass erupting from it and stretching farther up and farther in.

One time we stumbled on a house way up there, which reminded me that I didn't really know whose land this was. Bullet and I backed out and tried a different route. We found a valley or crevice between two hills and followed that up. We then found one place where there grew a grove of neck-high greenery, a sort of fern, that we had to wade through. We kept on, finding more inclines, sharp, sharper, and sharpest. At one point we found an old trail that curved around a bend of the mountain. It made for easy walking. Bullet got so excited about the levelness of this trail that he took off ahead. I had not been using a leash during any of these mountain hikes because, until now, the dog had done a good job of staying with me. Here, though, he ran like a redbone on a coon scent. I didn't really think much of it as he disappeared around the curve of the trail, running fast. Then I heard the barking. Not from Bullet—he never barked, ever—but from other dogs. A second later, there came Bullet, living up to his name in a way never demonstrated before. I had no idea he could run so fast. He shot toward me with his head lowered and his legs churning, and right behind him came two big, black Doberman pinschers. They looked like something out of a war movie. Beautiful dogs, but also intimidating, strong and dangerous.

They came on full bore, chasing after Bullet, but they put on the brakes when they saw me. If they had known how scared I was, they wouldn't have worried a bit, but as I'd clearly caught them off guard, I took advantage of the moment and gave a good yell, waving my arms and stepping forward. It worked. They turned tail and ran off around the mountain. I was glad. A dog fight—like the one at the beginning of Wilson Rawls's book, for instance—is not a pretty sight, and I had no desire to be a part of breaking one up alone and barefoot on this mountain. I turned back to find Bullet, and saw him strutting behind me like a prizefighter. His face spoke as clearly as words: "Yeah, that's right, you'd better run away!"

He and I pressed on a different way, still wanting to find the tip-top of this mass of mountains, but not wanting to meet those dogs. After several tiring hours of ascent, we came to a place where, finally, there was no more "up." Victory! Well, sort of. Even here the mountain had a final lesson for this boy from the flatlands. Whereas I had expected to reach the summit and have a view—the lake below, maybe even a piece of our cabin—that was not the case. Standing on the peak, I could see only what I'd been seeing all day: trees, trees, trees. I plopped down on the leafy ground. Bullet sprawled panting beside me. We had beaten the mountain but received no view in return. I considered climbing a tree, which would possibly provide the view I wanted, but none of the trees looked easily climbable. In the end, after only a short stay, we headed back down, all the while keeping a sharp eye for any Dobermans who might want a rematch.

Bullet on Lake Burton Dock

Swimming with Bullet at Lake Burton

Our week at the lake was only the beginning for Bullet and me. To truly be like *Where the Red Fern Grows*, we had to hunt, not hike, and back in Bleckley County I resolved to do just that. Instead of coons, which I knew nothing about, I opted for another animal often hunted with dogs: the gray squirrel. Though a stray and a mutt, Bullet did, with imagination and dim lighting, have the look of a feist, which is a popular breed for squirrel hunting. Plus, I knew a little about squirrel hunting already. Dad had taken me hunting all my life—mostly deer, but also squirrel. We had never used dogs, but now that I was on this new story kick, dogs were a must.

I began Bullet's training knowing nothing about it beyond what was depicted in the *Red Fern* movie, specifically the scene where Billy drags a coonskin around the yard and hides it for the dogs to find. Imitating this, I set my squirrel trap, which had been in storage since the *Redwall* days, and soon caught a big gray. I then shot it with a pellet rifle. I hate that part of this memory. The former Wes would rather have shot his own foot than execute Silent Sam, but I'd entered a different storyline now, and Billy killed his coons. See in this the transformative power of story.

Having done the deed, I dragged the carcass around the yard for Bullet to track. It was quite a trail I left—side to side and round and round and up one tree and down another and back again. A maze to make a dog dizzy, but I wanted to know how smart my fake feist could be. Reaching overhead with a hammer, I nailed the squirrel carcass as high as I could get it on a tree trunk in the back woods, only steps away from my forgotten time capsule.

In the movie, Billy's sisters hold back his two redbones

while he makes the trail. I did not have to bother with this because Bullet couldn't care less what I was up to. Actually, I had to rouse the lazy pooch out of the garage after I'd gotten the squirrel tacked up. I led him to the spot where I had started the trail, squatted down, and stroked the top of his head. "Alright boy," I said, as if he knew English, "there's a squirrel out there, and you got to find him." Then I stood and said "Hunt!" while patting two firm taps on his right side.

Against all odds, hunt he did. The fact is, Bullet took to tracking quite naturally. Perhaps this was because, in his puppy days, he had survived on his own for a time before we discovered him at the old farmhouse. Whatever the reason, he stayed right on this trail, at least for the first twenty yards. He then drifted this way and that, zigzagging off the path a bit, but always turning back when the scent grew cold. His persistent trial-and-error sniffing paid off, and his nose eventually led him to the tree where, looking up, he saw the squirrel. When he got there, he didn't bark, and I had no idea how to teach him to, but he did jump his front paws onto the trunk and stare at the carcass. Seeing him jumping like that felt promising. In that moment, he looked, by golly, like a squirrel dog. I was excited.

I played this game several times with him, and though I never got him to bark at the designated tree—never got him to bark at all—I was on the whole impressed. Finally, I deemed him ready for an actual hunt, and I told him so.

We had hunting land on the south end of Bleckley County, and it was there I did most of my wilderness exploring growing up. Now I took Bullet, and together we played our best version of Billy, Dan, and Ann as we romped around the shady forest of the Limestone Creek swamp. There were squirrels everywhere, and Bullet had no idea what to do with them, and I had no idea how to teach him. As I understood it, the job of a squirrel dog was to run into the woods and bark up a tree that contained a squirrel. The hunter would then follow the barking and shoot the treed squirrel. But Bullet, despite all his promise in training, treed nothing. He just bolted around the woods, chasing one scent after another and another and another. He never followed any one to anywhere. And of course he never barked, not even up the wrong tree.

I think there was just too much animal activity in those rural woods. In town, there were simply fewer smells for him to sort out, but in the swamp, the scents of countless critters created a sort of sensory overload in Bullet's sensitive nose. Also, the bloodstained carcass I'd used for his training was probably more pungent and interesting than the scampering of living squirrels. I hunted on, though, taking him out time and time again. What I soon realized was that squirrel hunting was fun in its own right, even if I was leading the dog to the squirrels rather than him leading me. The thrill of the woods began to infect me. To some extent, it always had, but now the forests were "storied," filled with the distant barking of redbones, the scurrying of the Ghost Coon, the scream of the mountain lion. I came to love the woods as I loved the story, and having a dog was part of that narrative—skill or no skill, squirrels or no squirrels.

A nameless, inarticulate suspicion was growing in my mind in those days. It was an image more than a thought, a notion rather than a distinct idea. It whispered something about days gone by, about old timers and old ways. It was the faint echo of crackling leaves beneath a worn boot or a bare foot. The pull of a dog on a leash. The rustle in a tree overhead. The beaver dams with their tiny crystalline waterfalls in the shady swamps. Cypress knees and magnolia leaves. Wind-felled trees and cavernous holes made by their pulled-up roots. Old wire fences, decayed and hidden like a lost city, so old their metal strands ran right through the center of oaks that had grown around them. Who built that fence? What were they fencing in? What were they fencing out?

This nameless nostalgia grew with each trip to the swamp. It was the reason I preferred, on evening hunts that ended in darkness, a kerosene lantern (the same one from my sailboat) to a far more practical flashlight. It even affected my choice of weapon. Initially, I'd hunted with an automatic shotgun—a Remington 1100, with a modern synthetic stock—but here I transitioned to my grandpa's old double-barrel sixteen gauge. Its wooden stock was discolored by the sweat and oil from hunters' hands carrying it over lost years. How many squirrels and doves and coons it must have killed in its time. How many stories loaded in those two old barrels. Bullet and I were hunting with ghosts.

At this stage, other narratives joined the swelling chorus of woods and adventure. Some were books, like *The Education of Little Tree*, which we read in eleventh-grade English class. Some were movies, like *The War* and *Sergeant York*, which filled gaps and rounded features in my misty image of olden times. Some of the strongest influences were actually songs, particularly the ones ripe with story. Never underestimate the narrative power of songs. They have shaped our culture as much as any other art form. For me, in those days, it was "Red Dirt

Road" with its walking to church and racing back, "Green River" with its barefoot girls in the moonlight, "Swamp Music" with its hound dog barking, and "Louisiana Saturday Night" with its possums and rifles and one-eyed dogs.

Songs gained a particularly prominent place because around this time I turned sixteen, and a vehicle is a rolling jukebox. The day I got my license, I hugged my mom, rolled down the windows, turned up the volume, and took off. All those dream-inspiring songs became the soundtrack of my life. Nothing makes a moment feel more cinematic than a score, and here, finally, was a way to be followed by music just like the people on the big screens.

That first day I took every red dirt road I could find. At one point, pausing at a stop sign, I looked over at the seat next to me and laughed out loud. After a year of learner's permit driving, always accompanied by an adult, I sat amazed that I was now alone. What I was doing felt too good to be legal. I drove on, passing an old one-story church, a cotton field, an abandoned barn. I ended up parked at the Dykes River Landing on the banks of the Ocmulgee. I turned the key backwards and blared "Proud Mary" as the muddy water rolled past.

Over the ensuing months, I stocked my truck like a wilderness man. It was a 1995, single cab Chevrolet Silverado, but I loaded it like an African safari buggy. In its bed I kept a water cooler, a sleeping mat, and a fishing pole. In the toolbox I kept a tow chain, jumper cables, tool kit, tackle box, and a stack of MRE military rations—"Meals Ready to Eat." In the cab I had my shotgun, an oversized Crocodile Dundee knife, a small squirrel-skinning knife, and a compass. What I thought I was going to do with this stuff, what sort of Rubicon adventure I expected to drive into, I don't know, but I liked having it all. The supplies fit my storyline.

Feeling the adventurous need for new and unfamiliar territory, I began choosing the Ocmulgee Management Area over the Limestone Creek swamp for my hunts. I didn't take Bullet because this was public land, and I was an embarrassing amateur at dog handling. Instead, I stuffed my pockets with sunflower seeds, loaded my double barrel with shells, and walked alone for miles and miles through those river swamps, trying not to get lost but secretly hoping that I would.

I came to be a pretty fair squirrel hunter—dogless now. I even gained enough confidence to start inviting friends along. If they wore camo, we would walk together. If they were less diligent and wore blue jeans or plain jackets, we'd split up. I didn't want them scaring off my quarry. It wasn't that I was qualified to teach anyone anything about squirrel hunting, but experience seemed to prove that camo was a significant factor. In truth, I had only that and one other bit of advice to give those with me. I didn't know where I'd learned it, but someone somewhere had told me that squirrels have a memory of only fifteen minutes. No matter how much noise we made walking into the woods, if we would sit still for fifteen minutes, the gray critters would start popping out of their nests and their holes, acting for all the world as if nothing had happened. I couldn't swear to the neuroscience behind this, but it certainly proved true in practice: sit still in good camo for fifteen minutes, and the tops of the trees will shake.

Billy Coleman lived for the sound of barking dogs on a coon's scent. In like fashion, I came to get a real high from the sound of a shaking canopy. The stillness broken by a rustling branch overhead sped my pulse. I'd be up in a flash and in pursuit, sometimes sneaking toward the squirrel, sometimes running full sprint till in range, then blasting up into the shake with my shotgun. Several co-hunters found this latter method odd, and probably it was, but at least it worked. Sit, sprint, shoot. And there was, to me, no sweeter sound than a single blast from an antique gun, then a silence, then a thud. I'd pick up the squirrel and put him in the pouch sewn into the back of my vest. I got in the habit of killing two on every trip—only two, because that was all I needed for a stew. And I got pretty good at making stew, though Mom never grew comfortable opening the refrigerator and finding two red carcasses skinned and flayed and pointing their nubbed feet at her. I eventually learned to push them toward the back of the fridge, out of sight, while they awaited the pot.

Two squirrels on a hunt is nothing to brag about, is downright laughable to a real hunter, but even so, I became a little arrogant about my hunting skills. That is, until one occasion when I learned how limited my marksmanship was. One of my friends, who preferred his .22 rifle to a shotgun, came along for an Ocmulgee squirrel hunt. In the spirit of comradery, I left my shotgun and brought my .22, which was something I never did. We were deep in some swamp or other, half lost and wholly happy. The river was a mile or two from us, and the lowland forest we roamed was thick with cypress knees. The ancient trees loomed high above. Our steps rustled the noisy leaves, and every animal in earshot was silent and still. The only movement was ourselves. We eventually sat at the base of a large trunk and waited on things to settle down.

"Fifteen minutes," I said.

I liked sitting there in the quiet woods, and it even occurred to me that with this new choice of weapon, the game of squirrel hunting was perhaps a bit easier. Whereas the range of my sixteen gauge was maybe thirty yards, my .22 could reach out two or three times that far. It could shoot, theoretically, as far as my eyes could see in this forest.

The only question was whether I had the talent to hit a tiny creature that far away. With my shotgun, I really only aimed in the general area of the squirrel—sometimes not even exactly seeing him but only the shaking branch—and down he came. With a .22, though, I had to steady, aim, fire. Sitting there, I began to doubt if this was even possible. Why did people hunt with these things? Was this really an advantage? I liked the idea of increased range, but doubted if a squirrel would stop running long enough for anyone to shoot him. Unless people shot them on the run, but that was surely impossible. A running, hopping, limb-shaking squirrel was no kind of target—this wasn't the movies.

After about ten minutes of us sitting at the tree, the woods began to come alive. We heard little noises here and there, some on the ground, some high in the canopy. I scanned the forest for any sign of a potential target, when suddenly my friend stood and pointed his gun right up into the very tree where we were sitting. I looked skyward, and sure enough, there in the tip-top was a shaking limb. I knew immediately it was a squirrel. But so high! Up in the clouds, and running. No chance of a shot. I wanted to be ready to fire if the squirrel paused, so I stood and readied my gun. My .22 had a scope, and it proved a real challenge for me to locate the squirrel in the glass. I could see him with the naked eye, but as soon as I put the lens to my face, I got disoriented. All I could see was the magnified image of limbs and leaves.

I was still pointing my barrel up to the clouds when I heard the sharp, quiet pee-ow of my friend's rifle. I had just enough time to think, *Yeah right, like you hit that little gray dot scampering around way up there*, when at that moment, I kid you not, a blob of blood landed right in my upturned eye, and the dead carcass of a squirrel thudded at my feet. One shot, one kill. I was humbled.

During this season of dogless hunting, Bullet and my mom grew close. Consequently, he became less and less of a wilderness animal, and even when I wanted to take him, he seemed unenthusiastic. He now lived in the air-conditioned house, taking long naps on a fluffy dog bed in the kitchen. Though he never said so, I could tell he found his new situation preferable to slogging through the swamps with me. I eventually quit inviting him. So it was that whenever I felt my *Red Fern* dreams reawakening, whenever I felt like having a dog to adventure with, I turned to another family pet, one that could be my pickup truck buddy, if only for an outing or two. Her name was Mandy, and she was my grandparents' big black lab. Conveniently, they lived on the Limestone Creek land, so all I had to do was drop by, load Mandy in the back of my truck, and ride the fields. We didn't hunt, but simply explored.

"Just be careful at the creeks," my grandpa warned. "Alligators love dogs."

One day Mandy and I cruised down a woody trail into the Limestone swamps, parking on the banks of an old fishing spot called The Jack Hole. I gave a look around for gators, then let her out to run and splash. The sun was hot, and the yellow flies were as big as marbles, but still it was a good time. Sure, she wasn't my dog, but the moment fit the narrative, and I was happy. I loaded her up again, and we rode some more, eventually coming to the large irrigation pond on the far side of the property. Here I decided to go exploring in the little aluminum boat Dad kept on the banks by the pump. Mandy was a bit too big for this small craft, so I opted to just let her play around on the bank while I paddled in the pond. I took my shotgun out of the rack in the back glass and headed for the boat. Mandy followed, but was too interested in this or that smell to be much offended when I left her on the shore. As I paddled away from the bank, she took off with her nose to the ground.

I watched as she began meandering upstream, exploring. The farmer who used this pond had, a few years prior, dug it deeper and deposited piles of clay on the edge of the water. The thick, craggy dirt looked like rubbled concrete, and sage brush and briars had fought their way through these dense stacks and covered all in a tangly mess of brush and bramble. A human's legs would have been sliced and diced on these banks, but Mandy plunged into them fearlessly.

I didn't mind. I could see her from the boat as she disappeared into the thicket, and I figured she'd give up and turn back sooner or later. It had to be hard going, even for her. I paddled upstream a bit, getting ahead of Mandy, but not really paying her much attention. I could see along the bank where the sage grass shook in the tops, meaning there was a black lab rooting around below. It was a bright day, hot and beautiful, and the glassy water reflected the white clouds below my hull. All was well.

Then I saw it. Ten yards farther up the bank, in the direction Mandy was heading, was a cleared patch of grass showing an exposed mound of dirt like the peak of a stony mountain. A thin scraped place, like a small ditch or slide, ran up the hill in an unmistakable style—on the summit sat a gator. I saw his green-black bulk perched there, the uncontested king of the Georgia jungle. His thick jaws bulged under his prehistoric eyes. His spiked tail extended out of sight behind him, then curled back so that I could see its tip pointing toward me. His claws lay large on the hardened clay. He was warming in the sun. Mandy didn't see him.

My grandpa's words came immediately to mind. I pictured what would happen if Mandy continued much farther. I stood up in the boat, and when I did, the gator raised his head and rolled open his eyelids. His fat belly stuck out like the midsection of a bull. He was roughly the same length as my boat, and under any other circumstances, I would have preferred him to stay where he was, where I could see him, rather than to slide invisibly under the black water where I could not. But Mandy was in danger, so I hollered at the gator.

He raised his head higher, and his tail began to slither like a snake. His short arms extended so that the bulky belly raised a bit off the clay. I yelled again, but he didn't move. I then yelled to Mandy to get back. She didn't flee. I reached down for my shotgun, the boat tipping and sending ripples off in both directions, marring the peaceful clouds in the sky's inverted reflection. I pointed the barrel at the gator, not at all wanting to shoot it, but thinking fast about what else I could do. Mandy was close now, but there was just enough space between her and him that I felt I could fire a shot between them and hopefully scare both off in opposite directions.

BOOM! The gun rumbled, pushing me back a bit, and shaking the boat. It worked. Mandy took off toward the truck, and the gator darted down the dirt slide, toward me. Gators are fat and short legged, but quick as cheetahs in short bursts, and he slipped into the water like a squirrel to his nest. He was gone now, safely away from the dog. Unfortunately, his invisible bulk was lurking somewhere below my boat. I traded gun for paddle and made quick work of getting to shore. Back in the truck, I knew it was high time to get Mandy home. This encounter was a bit too much like Billy's run-in with the mountain lion, and nearly as tragic. I resolved never to borrow anyone else's dog again.

Thankfully, Mandy didn't die that day, and didn't even know how close she'd come. Nor did Bullet ever come to any harm on any of my little adventures. Both of these dogs, two of the best that ever lived, spent their lives on easy beds with plentiful leftovers and loving owners. Thus, their ends did not play out quite like *Where the Red Fern Grows*. Instead, their own stories closed like so many good dogs and good men in history: one by car and one by cancer. They're both buried in the flat hills of Bleckley County, buried like two loving time capsules, and in our hearts, at least, a red fern grows between them.

Huck Finn & Dead Poets

Another story character who resonated with my love for the woods and my longing for adventure was Huckleberry Finn. I met him first by reading Mark Twain's *The Adventures of Tom Sawyer* in elementary school. I loved Huck's runaway adventure with Tom on Jackson's Island—living free, living off the land. I went on to read the sequel, *The Adventures of Huckleberry Finn*, but for some reason got lost halfway through and gave it up at the time. I revisited them both years later, in high school. Huck's taking off on a raft down the river, going who-knows-where, was the stuff of my teenage soul. I became obsessed with the mystery of the river, and I decided to build a raft.

Initially, I wanted a log raft just like Huck's. I had a vision of big logs, straight and barky, lashed together to form a large rectangle. I would install paddle-rudders fore and aft and a canvas tent on one end. I told my dad about these ideas, knowing I'd need his help and, most likely, his trees. He told me that rafts on the river don't work as easily as folks imagine. They're slow and hard to steer, and I'd be better off just using his aluminum Jon boat—meaning the one at the irrigation pond.

"But Huck Finn had a raft," I said.

"Believe me, if he'd had a Jon boat, he'd have used it."

There were a dozen good reasons not to build a log raft. One, it would require the chopping down of good trees for flighty reasons, and two, the vessel, even if I managed to complete it, would weigh a ton. How would I get it to the river? How would I get it out when the voyage was over?

I pondered these complications, and it was the river itself that brought me a solution. One day when I drove out to Dykes Landing, I discovered a flat, rectangular raft tied up along the bank next to the boat ramp. I was immediately mesmerized. The deck was made of plywood, braced by two-by-sixes screwed underneath. The raft's buoyancy came from metal fifty-five-gallon drums arranged under the plywood like two pontoons and fastened to the deck by ratchet straps. It was perfect in its simplicity, and it rode high and solid in the water. Since no one was around, I hopped aboard. It rocked beneath my weight, drifted out a bit from the bank, then tugged against the rope that lashed it to a tree. It was roomy and sturdy, and I loved it.

The raft seemed abandoned, and a wash of ethical justifications immediately came over me. I reasoned that it would be a waste to just leave it here, and that technically it was litter. If I went and got a trailer and loaded it up, I would be doing the environment a favor, right? Deep down, though, I knew I had to wait, because only time would tell if the vessel was truly abandoned. For all I knew, the owners might have simply run to town to get their trailer. They might be coming back for their raft any minute now.

Days went by, and I repeatedly drove to the river to see

about the raft. Then, one day, it was gone. I asked some of my friends, ones who kept up with river fishing and river happenings, about it, and though no one seemed to know who ended up with the raft, or if perhaps it had been cut loose and set adrift, I did find out the story of how it came to be there. Apparently, some folks from Macon—the big city upriver—had it in their minds that the Ocmulgee flowed in a circle. They'd built the raft and set off expecting to have a fun day on the water before eventually drifting back to the same landing where they'd launched. City folk. After a few days and nights afloat, the hungry and confused adventurers found themselves at Dykes Landing thumbing for a ride.

For days I'd wanted to commandeer that raft, but now the opportunity had passed. I did, however, acquire from it a new inspiration on raft design, and I set to work building my own mimic. A flea market in Cochran sold fifty-five-gallon drums, so I started there. They were only ten dollars apiece, so my overzealous mind immediately began dreaming of building not a raft but a yacht. Bigger is better! However, there was no escaping the limiting factor of transportation. The biggest trailer Dad had was fourteen feet long and eight feet wide. Those dimensions became the basis for my boat. I found I had to choose between two layouts. I could make long pontoons, one down each of the trailer's fourteen-foot sides. This would require eight barrels, total. Or I could put two barrels on each of the trailer's short ends, which would only require four barrels, cutting my costs in half. If I were making a motorboat, I reasoned, then I'd have to do the long-pontoon option, but since I was only wanting to drift with the current, it didn't matter how hydrodynamic the thing was. Therefore, I went with the cheaper option.

I bought the barrels and hauled them out to that same old farmhouse where we'd found Bullet years ago. The place had electricity, which allowed for power tools. It made for a good, unsupervised spot to work. Here I labored zealously for weeks. I used old four-by-fours, salvaged from a discarded swing set, as the main chassis, strapping barrels to them on both ends, and then strapping the wood beams together. This I overlaid with plywood—some bought, some salvaged.

There was a good bit of trial and error. Test floats in nearby ponds revealed some serious instability issues, so I added a few smaller plastic barrels on the sides to provide extra support. In the end, she rode high in the water and proved a solid, if cumbersome, craft. With that accomplished, I then added the amenities: an old sofa on one end, a metal glider on the other, a charcoal grill in the middle, and my favorite, a tin roof over all. For propulsion and steering, I built two long oars out of old drain pipes and tethered them to oarlocks made from a disassembled metal table. The finished product was something Huck himself would have been embarrassed to ride. I loved it.

I wish this story ended half as successfully as it began. Further test floats of the final design proved that the vessel was impossible to steer. First, the oarlock mounts were too weak, making the oars an immediate failure. I removed them and went instead with simple canoe paddles, but now when I paddled a few strokes on one side, the boat spun like a top, and I had to rush to the other in order to right its course. The procedure was unbearably inefficient. This in turn highlighted the most disappointing problem: all the furniture, though comfortable and cool looking, was perpetually in the way. Rushing across the deck to paddle was not easy when a glider, sofa, and grill took up most of the already limited space.

The raft was wonderfully buoyant and stable, but it would take a team of folks paddling hard to propel it successfully. This did not at all fit my vision of a leisurely Huck Finn float. I simply wanted to be chilling on the sofa, smelling charcoal and flipping burgers. Rolling on the river. I saw now that this wasn't going to happen. I voiced my defeat to some buddies one night, and they asked why I couldn't just put a rudder on the back. Let the river current provide the propulsion and a rudder provide the steering. This seemed sensible enough, in theory, but I knew better—I'd seen a movie that they hadn't. An oldie, *The African Queen*, in which Humphry Bogart explains how a riverboat must be propelled faster than the current in order for its rudder to be effective. Since I unquestioningly trusted good movies, I knew a rudder wouldn't work. I did give some serious thought to my buddies' other suggestion of simply attaching a trolling motor to the raft, but this felt very un-Huck-ish to me, and I couldn't mesh the idea with my dream.

So it was that my fancy raft ended up as permanent furniture in our irrigation pond, tied along the same bank where Mandy met the alligator. It never made it to the river. It didn't, but I did. The fever was in me and would not be denied, raft or no raft. The answer, I realized, was simple. As my dad originally said, if Huck had a Jon boat, he would use it. Well, my friends and I had Jon boats, and canoes too, so we decided to hit the water in these store-bought vessels.

We started with some short, unmemorable trips, just to get things figured out, but the biggest float we ever took, and one I'll never forget, was an overnight voyage from Dykes Landing to Hawkinsville. As usual, we didn't plan anything, but just decided one Friday evening that it felt like a good night for a real-deal float. It was already getting dark when we started hooking up trailers and loading boats. An unmotorized river float requires that a vehicle be left at the downriver landing, the finish line, while another vehicle transports the boats and crew to the upriver point, the starting line. All of this takes time, and it was nearly midnight before we got things in place and made it to the steep hill that leads to Dykes Landing.

The landing is usually pretty quiet, but for some reason this night had brought out half the county. There were tents and campers and cars and boats everywhere. Folks from ages eight to eighty were sitting around campfires or fishing from the bank or splashing around at the bottom of the ramp, talking, joking, laughing. At the particular moment we arrived, there was a notable hubbub of flashlights and activity at a spot right along the near bank. Someone mid-river had apparently flipped a boat, and a crew of self-appointed first responders was working to save the captain and right the ship, all without spilling their drinks.

As that crisis was resolving itself, we began unloading our canoes and Jon boats and carrying them down the ramp. Several strangers gravitated toward us.

"What y'all doing?" a bearded old man asked.

"Floating down the river," I explained.

"How far?"

"To Hawkinsville."

The man let out a quick chuckle. "You don't have any idea how long that will take, do you?"

I'd spent enough time on the Ocmulgee to be a bit insulted by his patronizing question, but I took it in good humor. "It'll take around seven hours, I figure. We plan to camp on a sandbar along the way."

This satisfied him, but right then our conversation was interrupted by two fellow highschoolers who had been hanging out at the landing and recognized us.

"What in the world are y'all doing?"

"Floating to Hawkinsville."

"Can we go?"

If I had said we were floating to the Atlantic, I think their response would have been the same. So it was that two more drifters were now added to our party. I doubt there will ever be another season in my life where I can, with no prior planning, drive to a river at midnight and find two buddies who have no qualms about floating away into the darkness on a whim.

Off we went, and like all river floats, the initial excitement and the primal landscape carried us nicely for the first mile or two. To set out on the Ocmulgee is to leave this century. There is nothing manmade on the Bleckley County portion of the river swamp through which we drifted. Not one streetlamp to be seen. The river, for all I know, looks just as it did a thousand years back.

There is a sharp curve to the right not far downriver from Dykes. On its outer, or left bank, a mossy cliff juts straight up for thirty feet, and there the trees grow. Their roots, digging into the soil, punch through the clay and rock cliff, hanging in a gnarled tangle over the water. You can find fossils in the dirt—old clam shells and sand dollars. Strange shapes this far from the ocean, but these are strange woods, and time ignores its usual boundaries.

We drifted silently by all this in the darkness. The trees loomed over us, a blackened canopy high in the night. The stars—far more stars than anywhere else in the county—glimmered through the open hallway of trees, straight overhead. They also reflected like drowned fireflies in the muddy water below. The surface was as flat as a mirror, and it held our floating fleet suspended between two worlds: the high and heavenly, the inverted reflection.

Past the cliff, a small creek stretches off to the left. When the river is low, this creek makes its trickling donation to the river, bringing rainwater from up the hill down to the Ocmulgee, joining the relentless flow oceanward. When the river is swollen and high, it pushes water the other direction, up the stream, up the hill. Everything in these swamps bends to the will of the river.

A hundred yards farther and there are rocks. Dangerous rocks, if the water is low. We heard them, that night—water cascading and boiling and bubbling over the shoal. The river was low enough for that. I knew we were near this stretch's sunken treasure, a topic of much conversation in Cochran. Large cylindrical pipes, half buried in mud, become visible when the level gets really low. They rest near the left bank, beside the boiling rocks. Some say they are the remains of an old steamship from the days when cotton barges smoked up and down the Ocmulgee. Others say they are merely leftovers from a sawmill that once operated in the woods above the cliff. Being a Huck Finn dreamer, I naturally gravitated to the steamboat theory, and hardly cared whether it was true or not.

No matter, for it was too highwater to see anything this night anyway, and we crept along past the bubbling rocks, farther into the primitive and watery darkness, farther into silence. Eventually, our party settled into the inevitable realization that river floating is, in many ways, a boring business. Every river floater knows this. Water and trees, water and trees.

Not that we were unhappy. This was perfect. The adventurous excitement, the good company, the varied conversation—it all helped us along. We talked and floated, talked and floated. At sandbars, we stopped and explored, then floated on. Sometimes we paddled, sometimes we just drifted. One of our vessels had a leak, and that also kept us occupied. It was a strange, paper-thin Jon boat we'd recently resurrected from a watery grave in a friend's pond where it had sat sunken for who knew how long. It flexed as easily as tinfoil and could only support one person. Every moment of our trip was backed by the ambient noise of a plastic cup scraping across the aluminum hull, this followed by water dumping over the side. Scoop, splash, scoop, splash, scoop, splash. We took turns in this leaky vessel so we could all share the burden of bailing.

We were maybe halfway to Hawkinsville when everyone was tired of this noise, emptied of conversation, and exhausted from the lateness of the hour. I remember hearing one of the two fellows we had picked up, last minute, at the landing. He sat in the front of their canoe and was yelling at his buddy in the back: "Wake up! Wake up! Turn!" Then, *smash*, right into the tangly branches of a willow tree.

Time to make camp.

We stopped at the next sandbar and set up our little tents, stuffing them with whatever blankets or bags we brought. No one had a pillow. We zipped ourselves inside, making room as best we could, and let the deep-swamp night noises take over. It was hot, and there was sand on our feet and in our tents, but exhaustion made up for any discomforts, and we were soon all asleep. The gators probably watched from the far bank, taking bets on which teenager would be the easiest pickings. I didn't care. This was perfect—a strange and wild paradise, our own Jackson's Island.

We woke early, and were packed and ready before the sun even topped the trees. Into the boats we went, away on down. We had miles left to go still, and this daylight leg was going to include summer heat in a way that the night had not. With the unshaded sun beating down on us, I began to miss my raft's tin roof. The heat, combined with our lack of sleep, made the former exuberance of the nightly adventure hard to duplicate. If I still held any idealized Huck Finn inspirations, it was with less enthusiasm than before. We floated on though, for there was nothing else to do.

Every minute of every mile was backed by the same ceaseless noise of a cup scraping across the hull of the leaky little boat. Bailing, bailing, bailing. I remember one fellow, taking his turn in this flimsy vessel, slipping into a sort of sleep-deprived trance. His arm moved methodically and mechanically while he just stared off into the woods and laughed.

Eventually, he swapped out to let someone else take a turn, and it was under the command of this new captain that the old craft finally had all she could stand. I'll never forget it, right there at a sharp bend in the river known as High Bluff, the flimsy little boat flexed a bit too much and dipped its bow into the water. It went down in two seconds, leaving its occupant floating and laughing. We made room for him in another boat.[1]

The final leg of this half-baked trip was nothing but a study in delirium. Somehow everything became funny. Every bend in the river promised Hawkinsville and not one actually delivered, until we all concluded that there was no Hawkinsville to be reached. Perhaps those Macon folks were right. Perhaps the Ocmulgee did flow in a circle! We'd gone loopy.

The day grew so hot that nearly everyone abandoned ship, choosing to float along in the coolness of the water rather than bake on deck. We kept loose hold of ropes tied to the empty boats. Mile after mile we drifted, until finally, mercifully, we rounded a bend and saw that beautiful Hawkinsville bridge. We'd finally made it. Our truck and trailer were there to greet us, and the river, once again, had given us the time of our lives.

Hawkinsville Bridge at Sunset

In those days, the river represented an intangible romanticism that was the undercurrent of my life. Its meaning was inextricably bound to some elusive symbolism that I could not place. All I knew was that a mystery lurked just around the next bend, just below the surface—a primitive, savage, youthfulness. The mystery was somehow wrapped up in the drifter's teasing longing to *not* stop at Hawkinsville, to leave no vehicles at the downriver landing. It could be done, yes it could, to just go, go away, wherever the current led. Life drifting off. That was the stuff of my youth.

A hundred memories beg for attention at this point. Tales from those days of the untamed, untethered, and unplanned. They must be denied. The theme of them all would be the same: if the seventeen-year-old Wes met the current, adult Wes, he'd snatch the little day planner out of my pocket and slap me with it. An incredible contrast divides me then from me now, and between the two, a chasm crossed.

Huckleberry Finn expresses this idea as effectively as any story can, buoying its message perfectly on the wildness of rivers. Countless other tales have chased the same elusive spirit in other ways. Some with rivers, some with railroads, some with highways, and some with youthfulness itself. I knew them well, back then, and understood them all. There was *Stand by Me*, with its trek down the train tracks, and *Smokey and the Bandit*, with its highway horizon. There was also *Saved by the Bell* and *Happy Days*, which portrayed for me a romanticized version of teenagerhood. And songs, too, like "Small Town Saturday Night" and "Chattahoochee"; "Ocean Avenue" and "The Middle." The list was endless—books, movies, shows, songs. All telling me, a teen, what it was to be me, a teen.

In fact, their lessons met me before my actual experiences. I was watching *Happy Days* before I was myself a teen. When I first met Fonzie or Ritchie or Potsie or Ralph, I was younger than them. Their letterman jacket, motorcycle riding, juke-box playing ways were the foreign frontier that stretched before me. It was a world apart, and its very atmosphere charmed me—the nostalgic past fused paradoxically with my own unwritten future.

In fourth grade, at our church's annual yard sale, I rejoiced to find a vintage record player that looked like something from the Cunningham house, something straight out of the 1950s. The sale was nearing its end, so the seller just gave it to me. It was shaped like a large suitcase, and the speakers folded in and latched so that the "portable" device could be carried —lugged, rather—by a single handle. It rode home with us to our blue house, and I set it up in my bedroom.

With a mild expectation of electric shock, I timidly in-serted its two-pronged plug into an outlet. Amazingly, the musty old player actually worked. I grabbed some vinyls from my dad's collection and spun them on the turntable. The crackling music that awoke when I dropped the needle intoxicated me. I fully felt like I'd stepped into a bygone decade. From that moment forward, I began having dreams of opening a throwback restaurant built around this single image of an old jukebox. My own Arnold's Diner. We'd have music and pinball, burgers and malts, and, above all, coolness.

Naturally, my actual teenage experiences, once I arrived, proved a good bit different than the televised portrayals. No diners, no jukeboxes, no motorcycles, and hardly any muscle cars. Still, beneath all the cinematic embellishments flowed an accurate conception of this essential youthful something that I did actually find. It was a sort of drugless high—life had exponentially. During my teens, it occurred to me, explicitly, overtly, and regularly: *This is the best I've ever felt, ever. And tomorrow I'll feel even better.* Tomorrow would come and prove me right. I grew dizzy discovering that this ethereal ecstasy had no ceiling, that these wild waters kept flowing, flowing in from inexhaustible, inexplicable headwaters.

On spring nights, we would back our trucks up to the rightfield fence of the high school baseball game, lower the tailgates, light a grill, and take the world in at a breath, only to casually exhale it again as if it would be there, forever. Other nights, we would sit around a bonfire, or on a bench downtown, or on the porch of the old farmhouse. Nowhere to go and nothing to do. In such moments, right through the cool autumn air, the distant cry of a freight train would reach our ears. My friends would sigh. They knew: time to get in the truck. I wanted to be there when the train passed the remote rural tracks. I wanted to see it go by, to watch it disappear around the bend, the tracks a rolling river all their own, curving ever away into mystery. What this elusive phantom was, I hardly knew, and no amount of chasing brought me any closer.

Then, out of nowhere, the phantom would find me—always when I wasn't looking. Once, in tenth grade, the feeling came through, of all things, a calendar. We were in third-period English class, and the teacher had on display a set of fundraiser calendars, with student paintings accompanying each month. I had a natural aversion to planning and foresight in those days, so calendars held no interest for me. But as a neighboring student flipped casually through the pages, right then it happened. The pang. The flood. I remember the moment so vividly, but I cannot conjure the feeling, nothing now beyond the intellect.

It was a hayfield that did it. Someone had drawn a hayfield for the month of October. What is it about the fall? That mystical autumn spirit, the cloudless blue sky, the warm and cold for one brief season meeting in perfect harmony so that the air feels like nothing at all. There in the October picture: the golden hayfield, fresh cut, with one lonesome bale. Feelings of fires and fairs, shadows and suns, blue skies and white clouds all combined to weigh me down beneath their blissful burden. Man's heart is not equipped to handle so much existence in so acute a shot, and my spirit buckled— the happiest of bucklings. Then it was gone, and the hayfield was just a hayfield.

The next year, again in an English class, we were reading

"Winter Dreams," by F. Scott Fitzgerald. Unexpectedly, there it came, the lovely lonesome stab. I knew exactly what the Winter Dreams were—knew it right away. The skis on the fallow fairways, the raft on the still pond, the melody of last summer's songs across the water. I felt I'd written it all myself and found my own time capsule. I lacked the capacity, in those days, to articulate any of this, and yet, here it was, inked into a story written nearly a century past.

Then fell the hammer blow. It happened the next year, in twelfth-grade literature, during our study of Britain's Romantic poets. Our teacher showed us a 1989 film entitled *Dead Poets Society*, starring Robin Williams. The dam breached. The flood came. I was transported. This, I felt, was me. I became immediately and irrecoverably obsessed. *Carpe diem.* That was exactly it! Our lives, like rivers, floated by each day, and the humdrum routiners of humanity let all slip by without so much as a glance. Seize it! Live! These became my battle cries. A new story had me. I was imitating again, yes, but something was fundamentally different this time. Unlike *20,000 Leagues* and *Redwall* and all the rest, here was a story that was actually about stories.

The film's hero, Mr. Keating, is a literature teacher, a lover of books and writings. The *carpe diem* side of *Dead Poets Society* harmonized immediately with my teenage highs, but it came inextricably linked to this fresh chord, this as yet unimagined idea that storytelling itself could be a calling. Nearly every interest I'd ever had in life could trace its roots to some originating narrative that inspired the adventure, some story that set it all in motion. Here it was happening again, but this time Mr. Keating was actually doing a vocational version of what I'd been doing all along. To him, the stories them-selves—the English, the literature, the poetry—were central. Greater still (how had I missed it?) the stabbing joys in my life, the moments of strongest ecstasy, had more often than not come in English classrooms. From hayfields to Fitzgerald, literature was the forest this spirit most readily haunted. For the first time, I began to pull my eye from the telescope's lens and look at the device itself. There I caught a glimmer—just the hint of a thought—that maybe this was the missing mystery all along.

It was only the beginning.

PART II

Mirrors

At a certain spot in our blue house, only a few steps from where I hid my map, a tall door-mirror could be swung round to face a large wall mirror. The first time I discovered this, I was enchanted. One mirror reflected off the other, back and back again, creating a long, infinite hallway of mirrors. Better still, when I stepped into the center of this feedback loop, the hallway became peopled with my infinite selves. When I raised an arm, a hundred arms went up. When I closed an eye, endless eyes closed. When I closed both eyes, well, I'm not sure what those unruly reflections did, unobserved.

Now imagine if somehow one of those tiny characters—one of those Wes reflections from far down the infinite hallway—began to wonder who his true self was. Impossible, of course, but the idea provides a useful entryway into the central paradox of art. Art is, to greater and lesser degrees, a reflection of reality, and humans are ever within its mirroring halls, but art also is, to greater and lesser degrees, a creator of the very reality that it is reflecting.

In my childhood days, stories propelled me down various paths, *creating* in me this or that interest, sending me on this or that pursuit. On the other hand, perhaps my inclinations were already there and the stories simply excited or inspired or, to one degree or another, reflected them. Take *Huck Finn*, for instance. Perhaps that book didn't actually create the adventurous youthful longing in me. That feeling may well have been there already. In fact, the reason I felt such an interest in such stories might have been because I saw in them a rendition of my own experiential reality. Notice how this rather turns Part One on its head: not me reflecting what I saw on the screen, but the screen reflecting, in part, what I was seeing in life. Well, which was it? Which came first? Where the original, where the reflection?

I remember as a kid having a mystical fascination with the night. There was something *peopled* about it, and a vague image of folks-still-awake shook me wonderfully. My childhood bed was next to a window on the second floor of our blue house, and I always kept the blinds open. We lived on a quiet street in a quiet neighborhood, but sometimes a late-night car would pass by, its headlights bouncing off the wallpaper in my room. In that moment, I would be deeply happy. Where were they going? What were they doing? People usually dislike noise at night, but for me, cars on the street outside or a television playing downstairs or a shower running in the bathroom, these were the joys of my sleep times. Folks up and about—I liked that.

A driver's license provided my first opportunity to find out what the neighborhood night owls did after sunset. City employees on street sweepers, nightshift clerks at gas stations, sidewalk pedestrians going who-knew-where in the middle of the night, these things fascinated me. In a bigger city, there would have been more of this nocturnal activity, but in Cochran there was precious little. So it was that I came to love the Huddle House, Cochran's only late-night eatery. Open twenty-four hours, seven days a week, always someone there. After Friday night football games, crowds would drift from the stadium to the Huddle House, filling the booths, the bar, the benches. Hours later, the town quieter, people would still come and go to the nearly empty restaurant, much to my amazement. Later still, the town now dead, at least one person would be at the bar or in a booth, too late to be a football fan but not late enough to be part of the early deer hunters. I loved it.

There was magic, for me, in this idea of people still awake, and so when I eventually met the corresponding artwork, my pump was well primed. I loved Edward Hopper's *Nighthawks* from the moment I first saw it. It was like a painting I would have painted if I could paint. An artistic projection of my own mind. Yet, it came from an artist I'd never met. How did he capture so well this unnamed impression of the night? The empty city street, the late-night café, the whole mystical, nocturnal, American thing. How did he know? I had the image alone in my mind, and then I found it reflected in the art, and the art in turn fueled and flamed my mind's longing. Or am I deceived? Had I seen Hopper's painting first, maybe without knowing it, on a puzzle box or billboard or something, and there began my longing? Or were Hopper and I both looking at some other, intangible, third thing—me pursuing it, him painting it? In these questions we see the reciprocating dance between image and art, between reality and representation.

It is a dance that will go round and round forever, like two mirrors held one to another, an infinite hallway.

At its best, it fosters a sort of consummation or completion, like me seeing *Nighthawks*. Even so, it's important to remember that no mirrors reflect perfectly, and some only through a glass darkly. Reality must pass through the artist's mind before it can project out again, and like light through a prism, some bending always occurs. In this way, an artist—be he screenwriter or novelist or whatever—paints a version of reality that not only mirrors but also makes. These artistic creations go forth into the waking world and actually bring about what the art pretends was there already. I am not here getting into the perception-reality problem. What I'm referring to is more tangible. It is simply this: people change their behaviors based on stories. Period. Teens end up acting like teens, as seen on TV, rather than being teens. Small town southerners end up acting like Mayberry rather than being, well, whatever we are. In its most extreme digression, an artist, bypassing reality entirely, will paint a picture of another painting, creating a feedback loop even more strange and disorienting than a hall of mirrors. The Rascal Flatts song "Mayberry" is an obvious example.

To complicate matters further, it's not two, but two hundred mirrors, for the art and artists are endless. With me, there were far more stories, uncountably more, than the selective samples covered in the preceding chapters. I ate spinach because of Popeye. Practiced dribbling because of *Pistol Pete*. Tried the crow-hop golf swing because of *Happy Gilmore*. Quit keeping score at golf because of Ty Webb. Took to sketching because of *Titanic*. Bought a decrepit ocean boat because of *Jaws*. Read *Auto Trader* because of *Joe Dirt*. I fished handlines with sardines because of Hemingway's *The Old Man and the Sea* and tried to join the military because of *A Farewell to Arms*. Even video games exhibited this strong narrative power over me. One night, elementary age, I quite literally prayed that I be made into Knuckles from *Sonic and Knuckles*.

My "Orca" (Actually a leaky 1971 Drummond.)
Cape San Blas, Florida

Is this sort of thing healthy? Well, on the positive side, much of it stemmed from my strong capacity to envision, and there is a real value to vision. Take again the example of the ocean, which is an allure I cannot credit solely to Nemo. Growing up, when I sat on the beach and stared at the water and waves, I saw something else besides. The ocean in front of me was empty, but the ocean in my mind was populated. Creaking wooden decks, rolling swells, low-hanging fog in the moonlight. A buoy bell, an island lighthouse, a sky of stars reflecting its inverted image in the depths below. I saw myself out there, before the mast, looking up at the constellations, rolling with the waves.

This was vision envisioned, image imagined. In it I found the joy, significance, and completeness of the ocean. Apply this principle outwardly to all things, and you get a pretty fair description of my life. A train passes through town and up pops images of hobos hopping on boxcars and riding away to their next adventure. A highway crosses a creek and my mind conjures images of log cabins built on stilts deep in the swamp, where moss-laden oaks hang their shady branches over the porch and yard, and cane poles rest on thick rusty nails above the front door. Shakespeare, not surprisingly, says it best:

> The poet's eye, in a fine frenzy rolling,
> Doth glance from heaven to earth, from earth
>   to heaven,
> And as imagination bodies forth
> The forms of things unknown, the poet's pen
> Turns them to shapes, and gives to airy nothing
> A local habitation and a name.
> Such tricks hath strong imagination.[2]

Stories played into my visionary capacities, and my visionary capacities enhanced the potency of stories. This is not inherently bad, and even when I would get so wrapped up in this or that story that I imitated parts of it, oh well. Mimicry is a part of humanity, and everyone imitates something. And if we imitate a thing long enough, it becomes our very self and no longer an imitation. Whether this is good or bad mostly depends on what, or who, is being imitated.

I say it depends on this right up to the moment when the mimicry escalates beyond healthy proportions. Eating can be good or bad depending on whether you're consuming apples or arsenic, but gluttony is always bad no matter what. It is a question of degree, and my special aptitude for envisioning did at times give stories, visions, and imitations a power that I was not ready to handle. Strength unbridled is a wild horse, and across my coming-of-age years lurks the cold shadow of imitation addiction, of unchecked mimesis. I don't know why I inclined so naturally, so automatically, toward mimicry, but I did.

Often it was story—Captain Nemo, Billy Coleman, Huck Finn—but not always. As frequently, it was real people. Many classmates unknowingly became my stencils, my role models. I remember on the first day of seventh grade, walking into homeroom and looking at a particular clique gathered by the windows, thinking, *Alright, this year I'm going to try to fit into that group—I'm going to act like them.* Fitting in, for this invertebrate, meant changing shape. Remold and remade, again and again. Another example happened during a high school gym class. Some friends and I were talking about music, and a certain Pink Floyd song came up in the conversation. I mentioned that I didn't like it. The reaction was swift and sharp, the group consensus unanimous—they all liked it. I was obviously wrong. For years afterward, and even when alone, I felt obligated to like that song, and even tried to convince myself that I actually did enjoy it. Another

Santiago Fishing Handlines (Notice the sardine cans and blocks of wrapped line. We didn't catch anything.)
St. Marys, Georgia

time, with different friends, a Travis Tritt song came on the radio, and I remarked how much I liked it, and was immediately made fun of—they didn't like it. I was obviously wrong. For years afterward, I continually reminded myself to dislike that song.

Half unconsciously, half deliberately, I took on this shape or that shape, making none of my own impressions. Rather than acting or talking like Wes, I'd act and talk and even dress like those around me. I wore a necklace to high school exactly once. A friend of mine saw it and said that he never wore necklaces, so that was the end of that. And the fact that I owned, in those days, a pair of Georgia Boots and a pair of Phat Farms says it all.

Truly, I wondered how my classmates managed it. How did they have such confidence and self-assurance? How did they know just what to say and just what to do? One answer, somewhat superficial, is that my classmates had been given a script to the present play and I had not. In other words, they watched "the right" movies, and I didn't. One time in second grade, I told some fellows who were horseplaying in the boys' bathroom that they weren't being civilized—a word I'd learned from Captain Nemo. Such things don't build a grand rep. My other scripts were no better. Whereas my classmates were taking their cues from *Ten Things I Hate About You* and *Friday Night Lights*, I was rerunning *Happy Days*.

A second answer, more fundamental, was that some of my classmates knew who they were and had confidence in it. They didn't need anyone's permission to be themselves. I wasn't there yet, so it's no wonder I made an impossible charade. It's hard to mirror a mirror, and the pool of my fluid personality proved overly adept at reflecting. The classic advice to "just be yourself" didn't help me, because I didn't know who my "self" was.

I felt alone in this predicament, but sometimes even the stories themselves indicated otherwise. Take, for instance, the Jimmy Buffett album referenced earlier. Track 10 is a song entitled "Pencil Thin Mustache," which is all about wishing to be the cool dudes on the big screen. Another easy example is when Richie Cunningham faces the impersonation dilemma, the mimetic desire, in *Happy Days* Season 2, Episode 4, "You Go to My Head." The show opens with Richie coming out of a movie theater and bemoaning how less-awesome he is than the folks on screen. He struggles with this issue the whole episode. He even visits a psychologist for insight on what it means to want to be the people in the movies. He goes also to The Fonz, who in a moment of great irony advises Richie to act like James Dean, and even demonstrates the procedure right there in Arnold's diner. Richie tries this on a girl at the bus stop, and she responds by giving him a book on abnormal psychology. The Fonz later rethinks his advice and tells Richie to just be himself.

I get it. It is a hard thing to be dissatisfied with yourself, because your *self* is the one you're stuck with forever. You want to be older but are young, or younger but are old. You want straight hair but have curly, or curly but have straight. You want to be tall but are short, fast but are slow, cool but are awkward. Looking back over the whole scope of my coming-of-age years, I see now that I was burdened by this inescapable sense of inadequacy, of dissatisfaction with *self*. And no wonder, when I, like so many others of my generation, held myself up against the fictional perfections created by the cinematic empire. Reality, with all its imperfections, can hardly expect to compete with these guys. All their auditions and scripts and rehearsals, their selections and rejections, their takes and double-takes, are honed and refined until the show is perfect, until the characters know just how to look and just what to say. They do everything right. Their lives are so central, exciting, adventurous, and interesting. What was I to all that?

Therefore, I mimicked, I imitated, I stole—trying to take what was theirs and make it mine. But this could not go on forever, and at times the symptoms boiled over. I remember one night, hanging out with a group of friends, fellow teen-agers, and growing unaccountably sick. Not physically, which would have been easier, but foundationally. I walked away from the group without a word, got in my truck and sped off. I drove into the night, out of town, out to our farm. I parked by the woods and walked alone along a moonlit field. I was near the same irrigation pond where Mandy had met the alligator, and I saw the pivot looming its silhouetted shadow against the starred sky. I climbed its mud-caked tire and got up onto the side ladder. I sat there beneath the quiet stars, with an infinite, chilled eternity above and before me. One unspoken question sagged in my soul like a stagnant pool: who am I?

The only answer was the silent sky and the inconstant moon.

One Story, Building

With a regularity as faithful as the tides, a calendar silently marked the rhythm of my young life. The academic calendars and athletic seasons were loud and obvious, but behind them all loomed the larger, ever-present liturgical calendar—the ebb and flow of sacred times and dates and years. I was raised in the Episcopal Church, and Episcopalians know how to mark time.

I remember that unique feeling of strangeness in December when the dining room of our blue house would flare with the strike of a match and the soft glow of the first Advent candle. Mom had a simple wooden cross that she kept in storage all year and pulled out on the fourth Sunday before Christmas. Large holes in the cross held five candles—three purple and a pink around the outer circumference, one white in the center. The white candle was the last, and was therefore charged with all the childhood expectancy of Christmas. Every gift asked for and every joyous longing, all the music of the whole season, symbolized in that one white candle that we would light—if the day would ever arrive!—on Christmas Eve.

But now was only the first candle. We still had four weeks to go. We still, at this official beginning of the church year,

were not even out of school for Winter Break. This one candle, a purple one, the Hope Candle, illuminated our dining
room table and shed just enough light for Mom to read the
Advent passage for the day. After the reading, one of us blew
out the candle, and the smoke rose toward the ceiling in the
darkness.

For a whole week it would be the same, this one candle
and a devotional reading. The next week, two candles, both
purple, Hope and Peace. The week after that, the third candle,
the pink one, which represented Joy. This was fitting because
around the time of this third candle came the release from
school. There is no feeling quite the same as that final bus
ride home on the eve of a big break, and Joy is a good word
and a good candle for the occasion.

Then came the week of the fourth candle, Love. Christmas
was almost here. Wrapped boxes appeared under the tree, to
be shaken but not opened. The packages themselves seemed
on the verge of bursting, as did I. Then, finally, mercifully,
joyfully, Christmas Eve arrived.

Our church celebrated with a true midnight service. It
began at 11 p.m. and lasted an hour. The church's Advent
wreath, displayed at the front of the sanctuary, burned all
five candles as we sang the songs of Christmas and read the
familiar passages from *The Book of Common Prayer*. There was
a story behind this season of celebration, and the church told
it faithfully, every year at midnight. We heard a sermon, took
Communion, and closed by lighting handheld candles and
singing "Silent Night" in the dark. Thus the service ended,
and we went home to bed to await the joyous morning, which

promised presents and family and food and, in short, the happiest time of a boy's life.

I was an acolyte in the Episcopal Church. Ours was a small congregation, but still we had at least a half-dozen other acolytes serving on a rotating basis. It was our job to light the candles, ring the bells, carry the cross, and prepare Communion. We wore white robes with sewn-in hoods, though we never actually put the hoods on our heads. A wooden cross on a necklace and a rope belt around the waist completed the outfit.

Regular services usually required only one or two acolytes, but for special occasions, like Christmas Eve, it was all hands on deck. There was not just the cross to bear, but also two torches, the Gospel book, and, my favorite, the incense censer. I remember my first time being admitted into the back room where the service equipment was stored—the wine and bread and candles and incense. We went there to light the censer. The priest taught us acolytes how to slide the brass lid up the chain to access the bowl. He then dropped in three round charcoal wafers, made especially for this purpose. He lit them with a long butane lighter, holding it patiently at the corner of one of the coals until it sparked and smoldered. There was no flame, only a soft red glow on the edge of one coal.

"Aren't you going to light the others?" someone asked.

"No, you just light one, and the fire will spread to the others."

"Why doesn't it have the smell?" Incense, as all Episcopalians know, has a sweet and potent aroma, but this was just plain smoke.

"Well," he explained, "this is not the incense. These are only the coals that make the fire. The incense is here," he said, scooping from a bag a spoonful of tiny crystals. They looked like oversized salt and were goldish-brown in color. "Nearer to service time, we'll drop a spoonful of these through the lid of the censer. That will give us the smell."

I was too young at the time to actually carry the incense during the service, but I longed for my future chance. A few years later it came, on Christmas Eve night. The priest—probably a different one, for they rotated periodically—showed me how to hold the chain with two hands and swing the censer gently back and forth, not only during the processional but also in the downtime awaiting the start of the service. "This," he said, "gives air to the coals and keeps the flame going."

I was more ready for this than he knew. The rumor among us acolytes was that certain priests would spin the censer back and forth and then, with a sharp flick of the wrist, all the way around, 360 degrees, during a service. Whether this actually ever happened or was merely a legend, like the ubiquitous playground myth of the kid who went all the way around on the swing set, I did not know, but I was determined to try.

During the half hour before my first service as incense bearer, I stood outside to keep the flame going without over-smoking the church. Everyone else was busy with this or that preparation inside the sanctuary, which left me unsupervised. It was the perfect opportunity, but I was scared. I swung the brass censer back and forth, back and forth in the cold December air. A little higher, a little more. It had a good flame now and was pouring smoke. Higher still, then, finally, with a snap of the hand, whoosh! Around it went. The chain never went slack, and the lid didn't pop off. Not a coal was lost. The flip had actually worked. Mercifully, I never tried this during an actual service, but I always liked knowing that I had the trick up my sleeve.

Of course, the full-spin theatric was not the point of the incense, and I knew this, even then, because I once asked a priest what was the purpose of this special-occasion censer. Why all this smoke?

"The rising smoke," he explained, "symbolizes our prayers, rising up to God in Heaven."

I liked that. I liked it even better than my round-about flip.

The liturgical year rolled on from there—into Epiphany, into Lent, into Easter. At the front of the sanctuary, on the wall next to the altar, hung a display board that always announced the current season. Some came and went without my noticing, but the ones that resonated were those that had a tangible activity attached to them. Lent, for instance, stuck out because of the pancakes, the ashes, and the fasting.

Shrove Tuesday, also known as "Fat Tuesday," is a night of feasting that precedes the season of Lenten fasting. On Shrove Tuesday, our church held a pancake supper. I loved pancakes, and at no other point in the year did I ever see so many in one place. My grandfather, a talented cook, served on the kitchen crew for the Shrove Tuesday meal. He and the other churchmen would make big pancakes the size of plates, and little pancakes the size of half-dollars. They also made sausage, spicy and mild; bacon, crispy and flimsy; and scrambled eggs, enough to feed an army. Syrup of all kinds stood ready on the tables, and toppings too—strawberries and blueberries and whipped cream. We kids got to be the first through the serving line in the social hall, our plates piled high with whatever we wanted. Food flowed freely on this night. I ate to the point of sickness and then went back for more.

The following night brought Ash Wednesday, far more solemn, and this marked the official beginning of Lent. There was no food or feasting on this night, but simply a service in the sanctuary. The event was made memorable by the part of the service where the congregants come to the kneelers at the altar gate. The priest would pass by with a bowl of ashes and rub a gray cross onto our foreheads, saying, "Remember that you are dust, and to dust you shall return." A powerful thought.

Lent lasted forty days. The tradition was to give up something, anything, during this season as a way to commemorate Jesus' fasting for forty days during His temptation in the wilderness. I knew folks who gave up caffeine or sweets or television. For myself, I only recall trying it once during childhood. It was sixth grade or so, amid a growth-spurt season of enormous appetite. In those days, I ate every meal like a man starved. Folks at school wondered where I put it all, for I was a wiry fellow, and they frequently joked that I had a tapeworm.

The standard portions of a school lunch were not enough for me, so I went into the middle school cafeteria each day with an eagle eye for light eaters, for those who might be willing to part with some of their food. "You gonna eat that?" was a common lunchtime phrase for me. Unwanted chicken tenders, pizza slices, macaroni cups, rice bowls—send them here! I took and ate indiscriminately. Sometimes even foolishly. For instance, one day the cafeteria served drumsticks, and as usual we each received only one. The thought of eating just one drumstick at a meal simply did not compute in my mind. I loved drumsticks. They were my bread and butter, my candy and dessert. If ever our family went to KFC for a bucket of chicken, it had better be a big bucket, and move fast if you want dark meat. Also, following my dad's example, I ate fried chicken to the bone, and then ate the ends of the bones. That white crunchy whatever-it-is was the best part of a drumstick. I ate them thoroughly.

However, on this particular day at school, with my one measly drumstick, I grew desperate watching everyone eating their fried chicken piece, not one person willing to give it up.

"Hey Wes," someone suggested, probably sensing an opportunity for some entertainment, "I bet you won't eat what folks leave on the bone."

I responded reflexively, "I bet I will."

Within seconds, a dozen partially eaten drumsticks poured onto my tray. I ate them all, setting a new record both for quantity and disgustingness. Amazingly, I didn't get sick from this, but it sure makes me sick to recall it.

Anyway, into this sort of lifestyle came my ambitious Lenten commitment: I would give up "extras." I would go forty days with only the standard cafeteria portions. I knew it wouldn't be easy and that I would be tempted, but I truly felt I could do it. That year's Shrove Tuesday, I ate an extra plate of pancakes in preparation.

At school the next day, I started my fast. Zealously and confidently I began. It was the first meal all year when I did not ask anyone, "You gonna eat that?" My classmates must

have noticed. As a sort of test, a fellow offered me something, unbidden, from his tray. When I declined, the forks
stopped clinking, the piano stopped playing, and someone in
the street screamed.

"What's wrong with you?"

"I'm giving up extras for Lent."

"What's Lent?"

"I'm not exactly sure, but it lasts forty days."

There was vague interest for a moment, then the conversation moved on. However, the next day, it came up again. An
eighth grader—that is, a middle school senior—asked me why
I wasn't taking any extras.

"I gave them up for Lent," I said.

"Oh," he replied, "well you know Lent doesn't actually
start until Sunday."

I didn't even ask for confirmation, but went straight into
"Can I have that rice? Send it over!" I ate whatever came my
way. The ensuing laughter told me I'd been tricked. It sounds
rather horrible to tell it now, but it wasn't as bad as it seems.
For one thing, the fellow sincerely apologized afterwards,
which is not something middle schoolers are prone to do.
Also, I was personally quite relieved that the fast had been
broken. I now felt liberated to give it up entirely and go back
to eating all the extras I could scavenge, which I did.

Though unsuccessful in execution, the process still burned
Lent into my mind as effectively as the Advent candles
burned Christmas. The story rolled on, and the traditions
marked the time.

The days passed, and then came Holy Week. Each year it

started with Palm Sunday, a day when the priest would bring a stack of green palm branches into the church. The congregants would then take them and place them reverently along the aisle, in memory of the branches placed on Jesus' path as He rode the young donkey into Jerusalem. We kids laid ours down just like the adults, but only after waving them a bit and poking their pointed ends into our fingertips. Childish distractions aside, the palms were tangible, memorable items, and our parents and priests did right to give them to us. It pressed the day into our memory. One year I particularly remember because mid-service the priest directed our attention to the baptismal font at the rear of the church. There he dipped a palm branch into the water and cast sprinkles over the congregation. He did this as a reminder of our own water baptisms.

Each year the palm branches, so I was told, were afterwards burned to make the ashes for Ash Wednesday. The poetry and ritualism of this fact resonated with me, syncopating mysteriously with some deep internal rhythm. It felt like something the creatures in Redwall would do. Even as a kid, I was moved. What was this story that caused these otherwise modern adults, folks who drove cars and had phones and used electricity, to do these ancient ritualistic things?

Holy Week continued with three days that stand out not one bit in my memory: Holy Monday, Holy Tuesday, and Holy Wednesday. We had no services and did nothing special on these days. Thursday, though, we gathered at the church for what was called the Maundy Thursday service. I remember it mostly because of my annual joke, "Why do they call it *Monday* Thursday?"

It was a serious night, though. At that service, we took Communion in remembrance of Jesus breaking bread and pouring wine with His disciples in the upper room on the night He was betrayed. Next came Good Friday, which, again, I remember primarily because of a linguistic oddity I spotted in it: "If Jesus was crucified on this day, why do we call it *Good*?" Then Holy Saturday, which I remember nothing about. Until finally, Easter, the first Sunday after the full moon on or following the vernal equinox. The day stands out to me for two reasons. One, because there was always a white cross placed before the altar, and the kids were given flowers to bring forward during the service. We inserted them into a wire mesh built over the cross until the bare wooden thing became a bursting, beautiful adornment—a living, vibrant emblem of life and color. The symbolism I probably missed at the time, but the impression made was strong and lasting.

The second reason, the Easter egg hunt, was less theologically symbolic, but certainly more exciting. Trinity Episcopal Church held a good Easter egg hunt. The night before, Mom would boil several dozen eggs and then get out these little plastic kits she kept for Easter egg coloring. I loved those things. We used a special crayon to draw designs onto the eggs —squiggly lines or loops or diamonds or a cross. Then we'd fit the eggs, upright, into wire hoops, shaped like tiny soup spoons, and lower them into cups of special dye. When they came out, the eggs would be the new color all over, except for where the magic crayon had been traced. The traced lines remained eggshell-white and thus created the design. The finished eggs were refrigerated until Sunday.

After Easter service, we'd gather in the social hall for a big lunch. Shrove Tuesday had led us into the dark days of fasting, and the Easter lunch gloriously led us out. There were picnic tables on the lawn, sweet tea at every turn, and more people in attendance than our church knew any other time of the year. After the meal, we kids, who had already inhaled our food and gone to the playground, were called back inside. We knew what this meant: time for the adults to hide the eggs.

The excitement in the room rose with each passing moment. Always some smart aleck, probably me, would sneak to the window and try to catch a glimpse of the goings-on outside, but the dishonest attempt was futile because the antique window screens of the old social hall allowed little visibility. Plus, the adults indoors would shoo us back to the tables, protecting the secret, until finally it was time to hunt. And hunt we did! There were eggs on the playground, eggs in the trees, eggs in the flower beds, eggs everywhere. Some were plastic with treasures inside—unwrapped jelly beans, tiny packs of Smarties, half-melted chocolate bars, a dime, a quarter, a dollar bill. Some were actual boiled eggs, contributed by the more traditional, or nutritional, adults.

The meaning of this ritual was, I'm sure, a mystery to everyone, young and old. There is no scriptural account of eggs at Easter, nor even a biological account of a bunny laying an egg. Still, we enjoyed it. And despite its silliness, the real story actually shined through in the end thanks to a conscientious bishop who visited Trinity one Easter.

In the Episcopal Church there is a ministerial hierarchy,

and a bishop ranks high up the ecclesiastical ladder. Therefore, his visit was a special occasion. In lieu of the usual 10 a.m. Sunday school class, all the acolytes were kept in the sanctuary to practice the service a few extra times. The bishop would be the one administering Communion, and we wanted to be in step with his procedure.

As the last run-through wound down, he invited all the acolytes to sit on the front pew for a little lesson. He held up an egg, which immediately grabbed the attention of all us young folks who were already thinking about the upcoming hunt. He then told us the extra-biblical story of Mary Magdalen and how she faced the emperor of Rome to tell him about the crucifixion and resurrection. She held an egg in her hand to illustrate for the emperor how the tomb had hatched Jesus to new life just as an egg hatches a living chick. The emperor mocked her, so she responded with a miracle. Holding up the egg, she made it turn red before his eyes. He was awed.

"And that," said our bishop, "is why we paint eggs on Easter."

Such were the ways of the church calendar in my childhood, impressing upon me year after year this narrative, this story of Christ, through the different liturgical seasons and rituals and reminders. Repetition was the Episcopalian way. Even the regular Sunday services reflected this. We used *The Book of Common Prayer*, Rite Two, page 355, every week. It was a script to follow, and by golly we followed it. I even remember getting annoyed with this in my younger days. Services, to a kid, were often something to endure rather than enjoy. I even voiced this complaint once at a church vestry meeting. I was certainly too young to be talking at such a gathering, but I blurted before anyone could stop me.

"Why do we have to say the Nicene Creed every Sunday? I think we got it. What if we did something different?"

The senior warden took it in stride, and simply said that those are the words of our faith, and we speak them so that we can be regularly reminded of what we believe. The answer didn't wholly satisfy me then, but I kept quiet about it. She was at least right, I had to admit, about the instructive power of repetition. Even at that age, I could recite the entire Nicene Creed as accurately as the script to *20,000 Leagues Under the Sea*.

At that meeting, I hadn't spoken up to be a smart aleck. Truly, I was curious about the question. Truly, I cared. The fact is, I was paying attention in church in those days. I remember one Sunday when our preacher, rather out of character, asked the congregation a question during his sermon. Not rhetorical, either—he actually expected and awaited an answer.

"Does anyone remember," he asked, "what I preached about last Sunday? What was Peter's confession on which the Church would be built?"

The silence loomed heavy. No one spoke. Until I answered: "You are the Messiah."

The preacher looked at me. I was just a kid. Then he said to the congregation, "We've got one."

I'll never forget it.

Wes the Crossbearer

Wes the Candlelighter

My interest in the things of God extended even beyond services and calendars. His story also reached me from the pages of a book. My first Bible was an illustrated children's edition. It had many pictures and few words. We read it often at bedtime. There I learned the classic narratives—Adam and Eve, Moses and Pharaoh, Daniel and the lions, Jesus and the disciples. One page struck me above all others. It was an illustration at the end of the book, the very last picture in the whole Bible, where the clouds open to reveal a distant view of Heaven. There were palaces and stairs and pillars and sunshine. It was hauntingly beautiful. The feeling of eternity struck me when I saw this picture, and it was a feeling that would shake me time and time again during my childhood. The weight of *forever* like a burst of leaden air, like a dizzying mountain peak. I was both fascinated and afraid. It had an alpine coldness to it, and a distinct loneliness. How could anyone share such a feeling? How could I explain it? It was just too bizarre.

For instance, in those days when the brief and powerful waves of eternity rolled over me, they were always associated, inexplicably, with Cochran's Highway 87, just past the four-way stop heading out of town by the hardware store. I don't know how or why that stretch of road wedded itself to my thoughts of eternity, but it did. Infinity, eternity, forever-ness perplexed me, scared me, and amazed me, all at once. One thing I knew: I loved that final picture in that little Bible.

As I grew, so did my Bible. In early adolescence, my grandmother gave me a grown-up Bible. In those days, I'd developed a special taste for books marked "complete and un-abridged," and so this real-deal Bible attracted me from the start. Plus, this one was all mine. It was new and nice and heavy, and it even had my name engraved on the front cover. I was excited to read it.

Thankfully, this edition was a study Bible. It included commentaries, definitions, historical notes, maps, and so forth. Most importantly, it provided several reading plans. I always enjoyed checklists, so I gravitated toward this. There were three options: a two-week survey of the Bible, a longer tour that touched every book in the Bible, and a straight read of every word in the Bible. This last one required three years. I went with the two-week survey.

I started strong, getting a real sense of satisfaction when I put a check in the small square next to a finished chapter. Soon, though, the momentum fizzled. Partly because of a lack of discipline, but also because it was too jumpy for me. A little here, a little there, but what was the plot? What was the storyline? Where did the pieces fit? My reader-mind couldn't compute this strange method of piecemeal reading. After all, I didn't approach other books this way. Therefore, I decided to try the whole Bible, straight through. This was an ambitious upgrade from the two-week overview. I made it well enough through Genesis, enjoying familiar stories of Adam and Eve, Noah's Ark, the Tower of Babel, and so forth. I also stayed strong during the first half of Exodus—probably because a *Rugrats* episode from childhood had already educated me in the story of Moses and Pharoah. But I hit my big snag in the dense forest of the Mosaic Law, in the endless statutes that extend beyond the Ten Commandments.

Exodus and Leviticus were not the best books for me to approach uninformed, without the wider knowledge needed to contextualize the Law. Not only was the reading hard and slow and dry, but also I misunderstood its application to the full Christian story. When I read the regulations of the temple, all those specifics on what to sacrifice for this or that sin, I felt overwhelmed. How could I ever fulfill all this? I remember reading something about sacrificing doves, and I began toying with the idea of dove hunting, wondering if shooting a bird from the sky counted as a sacrifice.

"Can we go dove hunting?" I asked my dad.

"They're out of season."

"But I really want to go."

"Why?"

"No reason."

I had a bad habit in those days of keeping my religious thoughts to myself, as if they were something to be hidden. In any case, I never actually blasted doves to satisfy the Law, but I did keep reading, which only led to more confusion. I soon stumbled into the labyrinth of Old Testament dietary regulations. Some were easy, like the prohibition of eating bats—no problem there. Some proved trickier, like abstaining from pork.

When I was a kid, a legendary barbecue restaurant operated in Hawkinsville, just across the Ocmulgee River. My family trips to this place were a big treat, and I always ordered pork ribs. However, on one such visit, after reading Leviticus, I shocked my parents when I ordered a hamburger.

No one ever came here for burgers. The best burgers in the world were on the other side of the river, at a barbecue restaurant in Cochran. Something was amiss, and my parents knew it.

"A hamburger? Are you feeling ok?"

Again, I didn't tell them what I was doing. I wish I had. They could easily have shed the New Testament light onto the Old Testament Law. As it was, I ate my hamburger, worried about my lack of sacrifices, and eventually—through a sort of spiritual exhaustion—gave up the dietary project altogether, simultaneously abandoning the Bible reading, mid-Leviticus.

When I finally, several years later, revisited the Bible in earnest, I knew from past failures that I needed a new approach. I decided to jump to the New Testament, starting with Matthew. This turned out to be a momentous decision. In Matthew, I found a cohesiveness and a relevance I had not seen before. Here was a narrative, a story arc, a plot. Journeys, mysteries, a pregnant virgin, angelic visits, celestial signs, stars, visions, and, at the end of the first chapter, the birth of Jesus. Then the Magi—wise men, coming mysteriously from the East, having secret meetings with a treacherous ruler, and bringing valuable gifts to a newborn king. They came to worship this child.

Then a dark and horrible scene of infanticide, followed shortly by a strange man, eating locusts and breathing fiery phrases about broods of vipers and axes at the roots of trees. This Bible, I recognized, was not the cushioned version from my illustrated children's edition. Here was fire and thunder. Here was a voice booming from above, proclaiming, "This is my Son, whom I love; with him I am well pleased."[3]

The narrative then showed me Satan and his tempting, and suddenly things got real. This was an arena that I, in the turbulent days of adolescence, knew all too well. I did not doubt for a moment the reality of an active devil. My own experiences with temptation and sin—a sort of madness, it seemed to me—gave enough evidence to prove him forever. And Jesus Himself spoke unambiguously on the topic of sin. From the weighty rhetoric in red, I learned that the stakes were high. "For wide is the gate and broad is the road that leads to destruction."[4] I felt that word, *destruction*, and shuddered. It was better, the red words said, to cut off a hand or pluck out an eye than to continue in sin. Serious stuff. I wanted to be righteous, but knew I wasn't.

At some point along this journey, I decided to take care of this sin business myself. I would, by golly, overcome evil in the name of God. On a simple piece of purple construction paper, I drew a chart of five boxes aligned horizontally, like a ladder tipped on its side. I marked the center box with a large X, representing the midpoint. Thus, there were two blank boxes to the left of the X and two to the right. I then sketched a frowning face on the far left and a Christian cross on the far right. Finally, I placed a dime, my movable token, on the X in the center. This all may seem like a strange activity for an adolescent who is simultaneously playing at Huck Finn and so forth, but amid all the narrative noise in my life, I truly did have a quiet, unspoken belief in those days that if someone really wanted to, he could actually live a righteous life. I felt this inarticulate suspicion, this wild and distant and primitive thought, that a person could actually live his life to God, could set off down that stream with no thought of returning.

At the end of each day, I would reflect on all that I had done and then move the token accordingly—one space to the left for every sin, and one space to the right for every good deed. The maddening frustration, I learned even within the first week, was that I could not stay ahead of it. Why this impossibility of avoiding sin? It seemed so doable, yet proved so impossible. As time went on, I also began sensing a fallacy within the chart itself—namely that a good deed doesn't cancel a bad one. A lie to one friend is unchanged by a kind word to another. A duty neglected at church is unimproved by an extra dutifulness in math class. Conversely, and despairingly, I came to realize that an evil deed *does* tend to cancel a good one. A single fib can demolish a lifetime of amassed credibility. It takes years to build a cathedral, but only one night to burn it down.

My purple-chart quest for righteousness was hitting as dead an end as when I'd thought of sacrificing doves and abstaining from pork. This was intolerable! I longed to know what, if anything, could cancel sin.

And then I met the Baptists.

I was in ninth grade or so, and a friend from school invited me to his church for a "Spam Hunt," whatever that was. He only offered the explanation that it would be a lot of fun. I liked fun things with friends, so I asked my parents if I could go. They said yes and dropped me off at the little one-story building on the corner where my friend went to church.

He met me at the front door, and we walked in together. Some of our other friends from school were already there, so we sat around talking until a lady directed us into the sanctuary to get the game started.

She explained the rules. "We have hidden one can of Spam

somewhere on this church property. One hint, it is indoors. One rule, it is not by that expensive sound equipment over there." She then split us into teams, guys versus girls, and set us to hunting.

This was an odd game, I thought, but at least no odder than an egg hunt. And anyway, the fun was in the competitive spirit, no matter the contest. We hunted hard, having a great time, laughing a lot. Eventually, someone found the potted meat. The female team, more's the pity. We could hear them all through the church shouting wildly as they rushed back to base with perhaps the weirdest prize in sports history. Our host then gathered us on the front pew of the sanctuary to declare the official winners. It was on that pew that I learned a notable distinction between Episcopalians and Baptists: evangelism. I figured, since the game was over, that it was about time to go home. Wrong. It was time for a message, a lesson. Spam, our leader explained, is an impure meat, an amalgamation of all sorts of other meats and meat products. God did not make our bodies to be like that, but intended us to remain pure.

The message was about marriage.

It must have been difficult to confront a group of young-and-awesome youth with a topic so dusty and dated as chastity. The movies of our generation placed sex somewhere between a pastime and a sport, portraying it as an activity for collecting trophies, not consummating marriage. Teaching about purity was like putting the little North Star against all the lights of Hollywood. Still, Polaris is brighter than it seems, and solid and ancient and stationary. It shined boldly that night into all our cinematic flashiness. It was a brave thing for that church to host such an event, and it was a brave message she delivered to us, one that further confirmed what my purple chart had already proven: sin was real.

Still, what could be done about it? That answer still eluded me.

It was around this time that my high school hired a new coaching staff for football, and these coaches were men who openly brought a Christian message as part of their package. We prayed at the end of every practice, and we bused over to local churches every Friday for our pre-game meals, which were accompanied by sermons from local pastors. One such pastor even became our team chaplain. Incidentally, his church was the same one I'd visited for the Spam Hunt. So it came to pass that one Sunday the whole team was invited, along with our families, to his church for a special service honoring the coaches and players.

I remember it as a moment of heavy world collision. Religion was my private world in those days, yet here were my friends and teammates from school, not in an algebra class or scrimmage game, but in a sanctuary. When the time for hymns came, I was embarrassed to sing in front of my buds. They would see me—all those people I was perpetually trying to imitate and impress. I held my hymnal and stared forward and said nothing. I'll never forget what happened. Standing silently in that pew, I snuck a quick glance to my left and, wonder of wonders, saw the toughest, coolest, most popular kid on the team singing like it was nothing. In that moment, an internal wall began to crack, and I decided to start visiting this church more often.

I attended regularly over the coming months. On one such visit, a guest speaker came to share a devotion with the youth group. He was a large, kindly man, dressed in a sort of Western style. He wore cowboy boots, which I remember especially because as he paced back and forth along the front pew where we were all sitting, he came down at one point on my toe. Yes, a preacher literally stepped on my toes. Figuratively, he came down even harder on my begrimed spirit. He told us the Gospel, that one all-important story. We all are sinners (I needed no convincing there), the sin debt is too big for us to pay, and God Himself came to Earth to settle it. He told us plainly and unapologetically this good news of grace. At the end of the message, he asked us to bow our heads and close our eyes. I figured he was going to pray.

"This is not between you and your friends," he said. "This is between you and the Lord. No looking around. All eyes closed."

Nope, not a prayer.

"If you know that you know that you are right with God, that if you died tonight you would go to Heaven, that you have been saved from your sins by our Lord Jesus, I'd like you to raise your hand."

I heard the movement of clothing. I wanted so badly to look around, to know the status of my peers. But this was, I knew, not about them. This was between me and my Maker.

"Thank you. You can put your hands down," the man said.

I had not raised my hand. That was my situation—and now the preacher and the Lord and I knew it.

He continued after a space of silence: "If you, right now, don't know that you know, aren't sure you're saved, can't say you would go to Heaven, I'd like you to raise your hand. No-body looking around, now."

No one had ever asked me these sorts of questions. The subject had come up in sermons and readings and so forth, but somehow it had always seemed vague and distant. Now it was localized and convicting. I felt, in that moment, just as Adam and Eve must have felt after the arsenic apple, when God asked where they were, and who told them they were naked. I was caught, exposed, vile—and I knew it. I realized I'd known it all along. The shame that had tremored in the shadows deep below ground now fractured into a full daylight earthquake. The sun scorched into a splitting and spreading fault line, and it hurt. I did not raise my hand, not for either of the preacher's questions. I was paralyzed. I'd been weighed on the scales and found wanting. No story or movie or imi-tation could pull me out of this one. My gods, my gods, why have you forsaken me?

After that night, I never again saw that visiting preacher. I don't know who he was. But I know this: I'd like to shake his hand and tell him thank you, thank you, thank you. He left our town to go back to wherever he was from, wholly unaware of the impact he'd had on me, the course change he had begun, the shattering influence of the One Story he'd told. He snatched me out from where I cowered in my hiding place and faced me up to the Lord.

What to do now?

That question above all others rumbled in my mind like the drums of approaching infantry. This ancient and invisible God, even here amid all the outward securities of the modern world, seemed to be drafting me into war, enlisting me to an inescapable duty.

Duty. That was the word. That was what I felt and feared. A relinquishing of control and giving over of self. It flew in the face of all that the world had told me. My generation had heard from all sides and since the beginning that this was a free country, that we could be anything we wanted to be. Now, seemingly out of nowhere, was this duty, this required action, this conscription. I could either resist and perish or surrender and join. I was outflanked—time to ask for terms of peace.

Here began a season of internal wrestling. Like the night I sat alone on the irrigation pivot, I again found myself seeking solitary places to think and pray. The Episcopal Church was, to my knowledge, the only sanctuary in town that left its doors unlocked, a bold welcome for anyone who needed to pray. More than once, this adolescent nighthawk glided into this darkened cubby and perched at the altar. The pale glow of moonlight through the stained-glass window illuminated my downturned face as I knelt there silently. Who am I, and what am I to do?

Jesus promised, "Ask and it will be given to you; seek and you will find; knock and the door will be opened to you."[5] The answer was right there, darkly, in the glass, but I did not yet have eyes to see. Not until my door finally opened one Sunday morning, back with the Baptists at a regular 11 a.m. service. It was there, with Christ in one ear and all my doubts in the other, that the Gospel got me. This One Story that had been growing all along, often without my knowing it. The answer in the glass. An answer that had even been on my old purple chart, though I'd not understood it. The very symbol I'd drawn on the right side, the cross, which I'd put there merely as a convenient emblem of goodness, I now saw as the great climax, the Alpha and Omega.

The pastor, our team chaplain, rolled on with his sermon as the Kingdom of Heaven rolled down to my ears. "Come to the Cross," he said. "There the price of your sin was paid. Will you accept Jesus' sacrifice? Come to the Cross!"

The One Story swelled to ripeness in my ears and heart and mind. It took me there in wholesale surrender. Church-goers talk of how it sometimes feels "like the preacher is preaching directly to me." That was exactly it! Through the preacher, the Holy Spirit, the Living God, did actually speak to me, divinely and directly. The experience was the exact inverse of the *story* influence typical of the rest of my life. Here I was not an onlooker or reader or viewer, but the protagonist himself, face to face with the adventure—the duty—that lay before me. This was a moment for Wes only. No one, not Nemo or Billy Coleman or Huck Finn, could help me here. No more charade, only hard and bare reality. I was not offered an imitation, but a summons. All the ground had been covered, and all the emptiness, vileness, and lostness brought to light. Now was a time to act. Something must be done. The beginning, middle, and end, the rising action and the climax, all contained in the stark simplicity of: "Come, follow me."[6]

I only vaguely understood what an altar call was, but like the physician's yank that removes the thorn or sets the bone, I ripped myself from the pew and walked, dizzily and surreally, down the aisle. I did not even feel worthy of the altar steps, but went instead to the far-right side to kneel by the piano, just as "the tax collector stood at a distance."[7]

God, have mercy on me. Have mercy on this sinner.

Does salvation come in a gradual enlightening or in a single flashing moment? God knows, and I trust He works it uniquely and perfectly in whosoever will. For me, at least, the answer was *both*. I had gradually been growing nearer to God for years, since the very beginning. All those liturgical days in the Episcopal Church, all the bedtime Bible stories and annual Advent candles—these mustard seeds found soil and grew with the imperceptible slowness of nature. Salvation came gradually. However, it also came in a flash, a bolt of lightning amid the darkness. There at the piano, a crisis and climax, an invasion of the Lord Jesus and a surrendering to Him. My sinful city had been besieged for a lifetime, but also the wall fell in a single, decisive moment.

Incidentally, no one had ever specified what to do afterwards. A born-and-raised Baptist would have known the drill. Approach the preacher, tell him about your decision, let him announce it to the church, and then be admitted as a new member upon your profession of faith and intention to be baptized. This is a good and proper procedure. Not knowing it, I simply went back to my pew.

In a way, I'm glad I didn't know what to do. It at least spared me the pitfall of choosing tradition over substance. There was no going-through-the-motions for me. There couldn't have been, because I didn't know what the motions were. All I knew was that I had been changed, that I was returning to my pew not the same man as when I had left it minutes before. I had enlisted, signed the papers, and sweetly surrendered.

Life's major moments are not always marked by proportional fanfare, and on the day my whole universe inverted, folks simply strolled away to lunch, whereas I had tasted and seen that the Lord is good.

I was baptized a few weeks later, lowered toward the clear water until my solid self met its rippled reflection—plunged in, fully covered. I went quietly down and up again. Pomp and parade might have carried connotations of a sprint, but what I'd embarked on was a pilgrimage: "Suppose one of you wants to build a tower. Won't you first sit down and estimate the cost to see if you have enough money to complete it?"[8] This dying to myself, this end of me, was more truly a beginning, the start of a lifelong construction project. I was new born, and saw already that this One Story was here to stay. It had shattered the mirrors in a decisive, dramatic smashing, and now it quietly prepared to help me navigate reality.

Re-Storied

The process was a slow and gradual coming into focus. It was like the blind man Jesus healed with the mud. After the first application, his vision came partially, with people appearing "like trees walking around."[9] When Jesus touched his eyes a second time, the man's sight was fully restored. So too with my life, for only incrementally did the spring of living water dissipate the sludge in my reflecting pool. In the growing clarity, I began—I begin—to see me.

Christ hit my imitation-laden life with a simple and unequivocal command, one that I had been violating from the start: "You shall not covet."[10] Envisioning was one thing, but envying was sin. This new light exposed the shadowy specter of envy and ego, the prideful mind of a man who is not content for someone else to be great, central, and awesome, but demands that *I* be great, central, and awesome. I grew to recognize my vain inability to applaud for someone else, and the corresponding impossibility of being satisfied with myself. I was wrong, covetously wrong, to trade up my present self again and again for new and better models, to be so ill-contented with me and mine that any other self I saw on screen would toss me into new imitations. This character today, that character tomorrow, but where did they all leave me? Further and further from myself, more and more a charade. I'd spent my life idolizing everyone else, yet somehow overlooked the latent idolatry in the whole operation.

Truly, Christ inverted everything. Against all my imperfections and inadequacies, the One Story lovingly whispered, "You are mine, and that is enough." God knows me, and He knew me even before I was formed. The very hairs on my head are numbered. What a thought! Made from the start in the image of God, and "conformed to the image of his Son" day after day.[11] What other validation does a body need? Of all the things I'm grateful for in my walk with the Lord, one of the greatest is that He showed me the two legs, my very own, that had been below me all along. Jesus said to me, just as to the paralytic, "Get up! Pick up your mat and walk."[12] Time to be yourself, Wes. Time to be a man.

What, then, of stories? Have I abandoned them? Not at all. True, I gave up everything to be born again, but I've somehow received it all back, washed and made new. I may be no longer childish, but I'm all the more childlike. When I first read Captain Joshua Slocum's *Sailing Alone Around the World*, I bought another sailboat. I was twenty-eight. When I first read James Michener's *Tales of the South Pacific*, that very weekend I lit a bonfire in the yard and cooked steaks over the open coals. I was thirty-one. When I read G. K. Chesterton's *Manalive*, I climbed a tree, still in my shirt and tie from a day of teaching school. I was thirty-three. To this day, whenever my neighbor comes over while I'm doing yard work, I consciously imitate the Robert Frost poem, "A Time to Talk," quoting it in my head.

What this shows—what I hope this whole memoir has shown—is that stories change our behaviors. Far from being a mere pastime, the narratives we internalize, and especially the ones we share collectively, are of utmost pragmatic importance. They tell us whether we should build a bomb or a bridge, a tank or a tractor, an arsenal or an altar. Most folks know this partially, but not fully. Everyone seems to keep a sharp and distrustful eye out for propaganda (e.g., Superman selling war bonds), but somehow we miss the pervading influence of stories in general (e.g., Superman misdefining manhood). Either way, the narratives are central, for good or ill. All the best stories, rightly taken, can contribute to the collective understanding of our human experience, can bring out the best and boldest of who we are and who we want to be. Conversely, the worst stories can derail us.

I have not escaped *story*—no one can. The difference between the old Wes and the new is that I now recognize mirrors as mirrors, stories as stories. That is, I approach reading and viewing with an awareness that I am reading and viewing. *Dead Poets Society* gave me a glimpse of this concept, taking my eye off the telescope, but God and growth have since schooled me thoroughly. A great portion of a narrative's intoxicating potency is taken away once the receiver recognizes that it is, after all, a work of art, that it is make-believe. This is the key to breaking the wild horse, reining it in and making it safe and useful. Most folks, even young children, know intellectually the divide between real and make-believe, but we do not always get it viscerally. If you had asked me in second grade, "Is Captain Nemo a real person," of course I would have said no, but only in the same way that a kid would say the Boogeyman is not a real creature when the closet door gets left open at bedtime.

The distinction is not so clear in the heart as it might appear in the head. The fact that I actually prayed to be Knuckles says a great deal. The fact that a kid once jumped out of a window playing Superman says a great deal more. Fred Rogers, who made five superhero episodes in reaction to such tragedies, was wise to stress in *Mr. Rogers' Neighborhood* the divide between reality and make-believe.[13] If this all seems a bit extreme, know that I nearly met my own end in like fashion. Impersonating WWF's "The Undertaker," who slept in a casket, I once tried to spend a night in my closed-lid toy chest. Thankfully, my parents found me after only a short while, though already I was sweaty and lightheaded.

Kids need help seeing the divide, and until they do, they are uniquely vulnerable to a story's message, whatever it may be. Plato knew this thousands of years ago,[14] and marketeers know it today, even if no one else does. A boy caught up in a story will readily pay for a movie ticket or action figure or branded lunch box, just as a grown man will readily pay for a boat or motorcycle or car so long as he has the right mental picture, the storied scenario, of a happy lake or distant highway. Just look at how Trans Am sales exploded after the release of *Smokey and the Bandit*. Yes, stories fuel desires. Add easy credit to this equation, so that the purchase can be finalized before the story-high wears off, and you'll have a pretty good picture of modern marketing.

The solution is not, however, to run and hide before the

narratives brainwash us. Sure, we need to be intentional about what we read and watch, and what our kids read and watch—"Do not be misled: 'Bad company corrupts good character.' "[15] The stories we read do in fact shape the lives we lead, so story selection is a big deal. But equally important is the trolley ride across the great mental Rubicon that recognizes story as story. We need to pay more attention to the man behind the curtain, the fellow typing at the keyboard.

Clearly, I did not approach stories this way during my coming-of-age years. The land of Redwall intoxicated me because it was, to my gut, a real land, just over the horizon, just through the woods, just down the river. In that dreamy frame of mind, I would have actually been repelled by any light shed on the facts of art and artist, fearing that the troll would turn to stone in the daylight. I remember one time stumbling on an old clip of Andy Griffith, dressed and in character as Sheriff Taylor, doing a commercial for Sanka coffee. I was disappointed. Up until that moment, some part of me had always treated the stories from Mayberry as a sort of documentary. When I saw this advertisement, a seismic plate shifted.

Sanka did me good, though, and helped wake me up. Humans need this awakening, this training in knowing what art is and how to take it. There's a reason we have literature classes in school. Happily, this training, this Rubicon, doesn't actually ruin the stories. Quite the opposite. To immerse into a story as my young self did, treating the events as if they were real, is to have the narrative only on one level. To go further in, taking a story as a work of art, is to have it on a new level without losing the first. A lay person can enjoy a fine wooden bed, or tree, or cave, but carpenters and dendrologists and geologists enjoy them as much and more besides—equally on the surface, but also below, on different and deeper planes.

When I came to recognize story as story, narratives as narratives, and all as art, I did not lose the inspiring magic, but only the drunkenness. I can now keep my sober wits about me as I enter this or that imaginative world. It's frightening to think that I ever did otherwise, and that many are equally vulnerable today and don't even realize it.

Sure, it is good and proper for art to be immersive—that is the mark of good art. A novel's ink should disappear in your hands as you escape into an Ozark coon hunt. An auditorium's adornments should darken as the play on stage draws you in. A theater's aisles should evanesce as the movie takes over. It's the poorly written books and poorly produced dramas that expel us out of the dream and into the waking world. I'm certainly not advocating that! But to enter art without knowing, both mentally and viscerally, that it is in fact art—and to do so in a world where technology is making our art increasingly immersive and increasingly ambient—is a frightening thing. In this air, we can easily find ourselves on the wrong side of reality without even knowing we've passed through a portal. We think we're in the real room, standing between the mirrors, when in fact we've slipped far into the infinite reflective hallway, unawares.

And how do we know this hasn't already happened, that we're not already in the Matrix? What narratives are we following even now, unawares, simply because they've been told so well or so constantly in our present age? Given the process of paintings mistaken for mirrors, of reflections mixed with reality, by what standard can we say what is real, solid, and original? The human heart craves such a cornerstone, and we sense that it must lie outside of the reflective passage. We can't keep telling ourselves about ourselves forever, no more than I can grab my own arm and lift myself off the ground.

The saving answer, for me, was in reaching beyond the fogged reflections and finding the reality outside the hall of mirrors. It wasn't in absorbing this or that chosen narrative and making it a part of me, but in giving myself up to a solid, outside, objective Narrative and becoming a part of it. Yes, the fascinating, reverberating, timeless point of my biography is that the One Story that shattered all that glass was a stone hewn out by non-human hands. One Story, hiding quite literally in plain sight, and proclaimed weekly in actual one-story buildings on every street corner. Too obvious to miss. Too obvious to see. There the Church, behind the scenes yet right in the open, telling the same 2000-year-old narrative all my life.

Wes the Bellringer

This may ring rather flat on modern ears because our age tends to gravitate instead toward "spirituality," venerating most the obscure and esoteric and *fascinating* religions. We are attracted to vague images of tribal gatherings in dark forests, festivals held on a certain solstice or moon phase—sacred times when the community gathers and worships its deity. We enjoy all this right up to the point where someone actually believes and does it. The moment this tribe gathers in a little church on the corner, it feels bland and dry and oppressive. The possibility of secret passages fascinates us, but the fact of a regular passage—right there in the open—only bores us, even if this regular door is the one that leads to the upper room.

We prefer the ancients, and picture them gathered around a fire, always with a good storyteller in their midst. He tells the tales that define their existence. Why are we here? Where did we come from? Where are we going? How should I see life, and how should I live it? The storied answers shine on the faces like the firelight, and the narratives frame their whole picture of life.

What I hope I've proven in this book is that if moderns have lost our fires, we haven't lost our frames. Storytellers still rule the world. The only difference is the mediums, the means of transmission, have diversified. It's the glow of a television screen rather than the glow of a fire, but still it speaks to those gathered around it, and does so with a dizzyingly broader reach. Yes, all of us are the recipients of narratives. Whether told by a nomadic minister or a Netflix miniseries, the stories come to us loud and clear. The peculiarity of the modern spirit is that it mockingly mistrusts the priests, whose faces and names we know, while simultaneously welcoming the screenwriters, whom we know not. What happens to a culture that trades the true and tried for the new and nebulous, time will tell, but let us at least not march forward under the misapprehension that we are being told no tales and that we have no priests.

The good news is that stories seem unable to escape God. Divine brushstrokes dwell in many a painting and are reflected in many a mirror. The traditions and expectations of our culture's story arcs, the archetypes and motifs that we hold most dear—themes of loss and redemption, hopelessness and salvation, evil and good—all are shadows and shades of the great One Story. I see it everywhere. Professor Aronnax plunges deeper into the sinking *Nautilus* in order to save his journal, which is his whole world, but Ned makes him save his life instead. "For what shall it profit a man, if he shall gain the whole world, and lose his own soul?"[16] Matthias enters the dark cave to face the serpent Asmodeus, and I remember, "Yea, though I walk through the valley of the shadow of death, I will fear no evil: for thou art with me."[17] Billy's dogs lay down their lives for him, and a piece of my heart better understands, "Greater love hath no man than this, that a man lay down his life for his friends."[18]

Even out of the fictions and into the facts, still the One Story is there. I take to sea in my little sailboat and remember how Jesus calmed the storm. I beach the boat and marvel at a God who said, "Hitherto shalt thou come, but no further: and here shall thy proud waves be stayed."[19] I see a squirrel and am amazed by the Creator's hand in all creatures great and small, and long for the lost days of Eden when Silent Sam would climb unafraid onto my shoulder. I scale a mountain, with a dog or without, and think of all the ages of mankind who have climbed mountains and built altars, knowing there is a god up there, somewhere, and of Jesus who climbed the mountainside alone to pray to His Father above. I ride the rivers and think of the Jordan that Joshua parted and crossed. I think too of my own story, unfolding day by day, flowing to me and from me in the ceaseless current of time, carrying me toward the final Jordan that we all must cross by and by.

Notes

1. Weeks later, a few of us returned in a motorboat to attempt a retrieval. First, I tied a large meat hook to a rope and lasso-tossed it toward the area where the vessel had sunk. Unfortunately, the hook flew off the rope and soared far out in the river, gone for good. Not to worry. My Plan-B was to breathe through a water hose while holding a heavy rock meant to pull me to the river's bottom. With this strategy, I could search for the lost boat at my leisure. (This didn't work, by the way. Well, the rock did.)

2. From *A Midsummer Night's Dream*

3. Matt. 3:17

4. Matt. 7:13

5. Matt. 7:7

6. Matt. 4:19

7. Luke 18:13

8. Luke 14:28

9. Mark 8:24

10. Exod. 20:17

11. Rom. 8:29

12. John 5:8

13. Episodes 1466-1470. To be clear, *Mr. Rogers' Neighborhood* fully recognizes the developmental value of make-believe, rightly understood.

14. See, for instance, *The Republic*, Books III and X.

15. 1 Cor. 15:33. Interestingly, Paul seems to be quoting a Greek playwright named Menander.

16. Mark 8:36 (KJV)

17. Ps. 23:4 (KJV)

18. John 15:13 (KJV)

19. Job 38:11 (KJV)

Acknowledgments

My eternal thanks to all who helped guide me to God. You are to me as the paralytic's friends who, finding no way into the house, tore off the roof and lowered him to Jesus.

To my readers: thank you for your time, and for any reviews/shares.

Thanks also to everyone who helped polish this manuscript, especially Penny and Russell.

And endless thanks to Mom and Dad for a happy and safe childhood.

Wes Young is a writer, teacher, preacher, and podcaster in Cochran, Georgia where he enjoys the quiet life with his wife and two daughters. He holds degrees from Reinhardt University and the University of Georgia. *One Story, Building* is his second book. Find more at wesyoungwriter.com.

Bonus

CHAPTER 30

Anac crouched on the backside of the row of buildings, hoping the agent had not seen him. He was well concealed here, unless the car came down one of these side streets that crossed the rail lines.

The tracks were ten paces away, and he watched for the approaching train. The alley was deserted, but to eastward he saw a large brick building whose parking lot was alive with people, several of them in matching blue uniforms. Must be the courthouse Tifforp spoke of. If he hopped the train, he would have to ride right past them.

WWWWWWWWWWWWWAAAAAAAAAAA!

Then, there it was. A large beast lumbering toward him, with glowing white eyes, and piercing, screeching breath. It looked fast, too fast, but he had to try. Staying here was death, and in Darien was life.

He stuffed the lure into his right pocket alongside the knife. He needed both hands free for this. The train's leading edge sped past him. His fear rose because of the sound. Horrid screeches and clatterings and whistles. His ears absorbed the noises as his feet and legs felt the rumblings. The ground shook, reminiscent of the earthquakes back home. He watched as the various containers clanked by. Some were tall and enclosed, the gratings on their sides allowing light to pass through. Some were filled with logs. Some were black and piled to overflowing with what looked like rocks or dirt. Some were flat and empty. One section consisted of nearly a dozen cylindrical cars, like giant pipes capped on both ends. He looked to the side streets. A few vehicles were pulled up to the edge of the tracks, parked beside large flashing red lights. He did not see the agent's car, so he focused all his attention on the train.

He studied places to grab hold. Each car had ladders on the sides and ends. He could try to jump on a side ladder, but he thought it best to wait until the train passed and then chase it from behind. Should he fall, he at least would not get caught under the wheels. Plus, both sides of the tracks were littered with loose gravel, sloping down two or three feet at a sharp angle. Not an ideal surface for running. If he waited until the last car, he could run on the flat space between the two rails.

The front of the train was now out of view, curving to the right on the far side of the courthouse. The rear of the train was still beyond sight. He then noticed that this back alley was no longer deserted. A man in a white cap and white apron was stomping boxes and tossing them into a large green bin. He was only ten paces away. Anac could see the man's mustache and a burning stick between his lips.

The end of the train rounded the curve. It was time. He made for the tracks, crossing a shallow ditch, his hurt foot slipping on the gravel as he went. Over the roar and rumble he heard a shout behind him. Must have been from the man in white. He could not make out what he said, but it didn't matter. The train was gaining speed with every passing moment, or perhaps it just seemed so because he was now right alongside it. He was anxious to jump, but knew he had to wait for that last car. If he grabbed hold without matching the train's speed, the force would rip his arms out of socket.

He readied. The last car shot past. He made his dash, now between the metal rails that ran along the gravelly ground. He sprinted toward a blinking red light hanging on the rear. The light was getting no closer, but no farther either. He was keeping up, but needed to close the distance. His run was troubled by the uneven surface. Large brown timbers crossed endlessly ahead and tripped him. If he fell to the ground, he'd never catch up. His injured foot was splitting pain now. He felt the wound had opened and imagined the blood that was in his boot. With a final burst, he let his legs burn all they had left. He was nearing the rear ladder, a shot of speed, searing pain. He lunged and took hold of the railing next to the flashing light.

He had it firmly in both hands, the cold steel on his palms. He was latched onto the train but had grabbed too low. His toes dragged along the wood and gravel. He jerked to pick up his feet, wondering how close they were to the razor wheels spinning madly below him. The tops of his boots were scratched and sliced by the rushing ground. He finally got his feet safely onto the lowest rung. He looped his arms around a bar and relaxed. He had caught the train. In this much needed moment of rest, he looked over his right shoulder to see the passing courthouse. His satisfaction was shattered by the sight of many eyes frozen and fastened on him. Among them stood the man with the bandaged head.

www.ingramcontent.com/pod-product-compliance
Lightning Source LLC
Chambersburg PA
CBHW010752150726
48196CB00008B/564